CW00665049

presents

Silence
by Moira Buffini

Silence was first performed in The Door,
Birmingham Repertory Theatre, on
14 October 1999.

Subsequently rewritten, *Silence* was
first performed in the new version, as
published here, as part of The REP's
Community Tour at Fairfax School,
Sutton Coldfield on 27 February 2002.
This production was also presented
in The Door, Birmingham Repertory
Theatre, on 20 March 2002.

Funded by
THE
ARTS
COUNCIL
OF ENGLAND

Birmingham City Council

WEST
MIDLANDS
ARTS

Providing Theatre for Birmingham

ᴴᴱREP

Since it was founded in 1913 Birmingham Repertory Theatre Company has been a leading national company. Its programming has introduced a range of new and foreign plays to the British theatre repertoire, and it has been a springboard for many internationally acclaimed actors, designers and directors.

The REP's productions regularly transfer to London and tour nationally and internationally. Recent productions include *The Snowman*, *A Wedding Story*, *Out In The Open*, *Tender*, *Behsharam* and *The Ramayana* at The Royal National Theatre and last year our acclaimed production of *Hamlet* played in the grounds of Elsinore Castle, Denmark as part of their annual Shakespeare Festival.

In 1998 the company launched The Door, a venue dedicated to the production and pre-sentation of new work. Through the extensive commissioning of new work The REP is providing vital opportunities for the young and emerging writing talent that will lead the way in the theatre of the future. This season includes plays by Kaite O'Reilly, Moira Buffini, Lloyd Withers, Lisa Evans and visits from Paines Plough and Shared Experience.

Developing new and particularly younger audiences is also at the heart of The REP's work. In its various Education initiatives, such as Transmissions, The Young REP, Page To Stage, as well as with the pro-gramming of work in The Door for children.

The REP produces over twenty new productions each year. Under the new Artistic Direction of Jonathan Church, The REP has enjoyed great success with one of its busiest and most exciting programmes ever. Highlights of the Spring-Summer season include *Hobson's Choice* (with Theatre Royal Plymouth and the Touring Consortium), Tara Arts' *Journey To the West*, the British premiere of *Elizabeth Rex*, the world premieres of *Masterpieces* and *Krindlekrax*, the community collaboration *Wallop Mrs Cox* and the West End hit *Stones In His Pockets*.

Artistic Director   Jonathan Church
Executive Director Stuart Rogers

Birmingham Repertory Theatre
Broad Street, Birmingham B1 2EP

Administration 0121 245 2000
Facsimile 0121 245 2100
Box Office 0121 236 4455
Minicom 0121 245 2025
www.birmingham-rep.co.uk

Silence
by Moira Buffini

Ymma
Elizabeth Marsh

Agnés
Joanne Moseley

Eadric
Nicholas Beveney

Silence
Maeve Larkin

Roger
Christopher Staines

Ethelred
John Flitcroft

Director
Anthony Clark

Designer
Rachel Blues

Lighting Designer
Andrew Fidgeon

Sound
Dean Whiskens

Stage Manager
Richard Greville Watson

Deputy Stage Manager
Ruth Morgan

Assistant Stage Manager (Book)
Philippa Thomas

Dialect Coach
William Conacher

Biographies

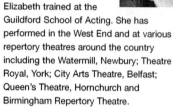

Moira Buffini
Writer

Moira Buffini studied English/ Drama at Goldsmiths College and trained as an actor at the Welsh College of Music and Drama. She acted professionally for five years, winning a Time Out Award in 1992 for her performance in *Jordan*. Whilst a drama teacher in Holloway prison, she directed two productions; *Two* by Jim Cartwright and J.P Sartre's adaptation of *The Trojan Women*.

As a writer her plays include: *Jordan* co-written with Anna Reynolds which won the Writers Guild Award for Best Fringe Play 1992; *Blavatsky's Tower*; *Gabriel* – Winner of LWT Plays on Stage Award 1997 and Winner of Meyer Whitworth Award 1998 (Soho Theatre Company); *Doomsday Girl* (The Other Place, RSC and revived for London New Plays festival – 1999 Gielgud Theatre); *Silence* – commissioned by the RNT Studio and Winner of Susan Smith Blackburn Prize (Birmingham Repertory Theatre and Plymouth Theatre Royal); *The Games Room*, a short play for The Focus Group (Soho Theatre); *Loveplay*, commissioned by RSC (The Pitt/ Barbican).

Moira is currently under commission to the Royal National Theatre and is Birmingham Repertory Theatre's playwright in residence (Pearson Television Playwright's Scheme).

Elizabeth Marsh
Ymma

Elizabeth trained at the Guildford School of Acting. She has performed in the West End and at various repertory theatres around the country including the Watermill, Newbury; Theatre Royal, York; City Arts Theatre, Belfast; Queen's Theatre, Hornchurch and Birmingham Repertory Theatre.

Favourite roles include Annie Wilkes in *Misery*; Beverly in *Abigail's Party*; Jean Rice in *The Entertainer*; Rose in *Brighton Rock*; Louisa in *Hard Times*; Suzanne in *Don't Dress for Dinner*; Rita in *In the Midnight Hour*; Felicity in *Habeus Corpus*; Rapunzel and Florinda in *Into the Woods*; Fay in *A Chorus of Disapproval*; Elizabeth in *Moll Flanders* (TMA Award – Best Musical); Witch in *From a Jack to a King*; Mme Giry in *Phantom of the Opera;* Mrs Kay in *Our Day Out*; Pamela in *The 39 Steps*; Fabia in *Twelfth Night*; Manuelita in *Carmen*; Cassilda in *Gondoliers* (TMA Award – Best Musical) and Winnie in *Winnie the Witch*.

West End roles include: Yitzak, the male rock singer in *Hedwig and the Angry Inch* and Cassilda in the critically acclaimed *Gondoliers.*

Elizabeth has also worked as a choreographer on numerous musicals, pantomimes and revues.

THEREP

Joanne Moseley
Agnés

Joanne was born and
bred in Birmingham and
was an active member of Stage Two Theatre
Company for eight years where she appeared
in a variety of productions including Viv in
Tom and Viv and Landlady in *Two*.

Joanne has also worked with other local
theatre companies including Maverick, Small
world – Big Feet, and Rear Window.

Joanne subsequently went to LAMDA where
she trained for three years before returning
home to Birmingham.

She has appeared at Leicester Haymarket in
The Crucible and most recently as Curley's
Wife in *Of Mice and* Men and *Private Lives*
here at Birmingham Repertory Theatre.

She has also made appearances in *The Bill*,
Doctors, *Peak Practice* and the award
winning *People Like Us*.

Nicholas Beveney
Eadric

Nicholas trained at the
Guilford School of Acting.

Theatre credits include:
Clarkey in *The Gift*
(Birmingham Repertory Theatre and Tricycle
Theatre); *Big Nose* (Belgrade Theatre);
Bottom in A *Midsummer Night's Dream*
(Oxford Stage Company); *Wicked Games*
(West Yorkshire Playhouse).

Television credits include: *Sir Gadabout*
(Alibi Productions); *Lock Stock . . .* (Ginger
Productions); *Trial and Retribution* (La Plante
Productions); *The Bill – Riot City* (Pearson

TV); *Maisie Raine* (BBC); *Pie in the Sky*
(SelecTV); *Turning World* (World Productions);
The Bill – Love Me Love My Dog (Thames
TV); *Respect* (Yorkshire Television); *Three
Ways in Myopic Man* (Channel 4); *Holding
on* (BBC2).

Film credits include: *The Fifth Element*
(Zaltman Films); *Jack and the Beanstalk* (Jim
Henson Productions).

Radio credits include: *Joys of War* and *The
Grass Is Singing* (BBC World Service).

He now has a production company 'Highrise
Media' specialising in pop promos and music
production.

Maeve Larkin
Silence

Theatre credits include:
Moll in *Moll Flanders*
(Dukes, Lancaster/Tour);
Cinderella and *Rebecca*
(Oldham Coliseum); *Don Quixote* (Dukes,
Lancaster, Park); *Seagulls* and *Princess
Sharon* (Scarlet Theatre and Polish Tour);
The Snow Queen (Lawrence Batley,
Huddersfield); *The Comedy of Errors*
(RSC/Young Vic); Little Voice in *Rise and Fall
of Little Voice* and *The Railway Children*
(Wolsey Theatre, Ipswich); *Engaged* and
What The Butler Saw (Perth Theatre);
Widower's Houses (Shaw's Corner); *A
Christmas Carol* (New Vic, Stoke); Mowgli
in *Jungle Book* (Tricycle Theatre and Tour);
The Fruit Has Turned To Jam (Young Vic
and Tour).

Television credits include: *Coronation Street*
and *Forsyte Saga* (Granada); *London's
Burning* (LWT); *Newsnight* (BBC).

Radio includes: *The Red Balloon* (BBC Radio 4).

Biographies

Christopher Staines
Roger

Theatre credits include:
The Three Sisters
(Chichester Festival Theatre); *Hamlet*
(Royal National Theatre); *Gross Indecency –
The Three Trials Of Oscar Wilde* (Theatre
Royal Plymouth and Gielgud Theatre West
End); *Amy's View* (National Theatre and
West End); *Leonce and Lena* (The Gate
Theatre); *The Belle Vue* (ATC); *Simpleton
of the Unexpected Isles, The Memorandum,
Portrait of a Woman* and *Flora The Red
Menace* (Orange Tree Theatre); *Richard III,
A Midsummer Night's Dream, The Music Man*
(Regents Park Open Air); *Cabaret* (Donmar
Warehouse); *An Evening With Gary Lineker*
(Royal Theatre, Northampton).

Television credits include: *The Student
Prince; Pride and Prejudice; Highlander;
This Life; The Queen's Nose; The Ruby Ring;
Good Friday 1663.*

Film credits include: *Mrs Dalloway.*

Radio credits include: *Dossier Ronald
Akkerman; The Rose and the Ring; The
Charm Factory; The Decameron; Antigone.*

John Flitcroft
Ethelred

After working as a
woodsman in the Lake
District and a law clerk in Leamington Spa,
John became an actor with local theatre
company, Pentabus. He appeared in over
sixteen of their productions including *Becca's
Children* and *Dancing with the Devil* and
returned last year to play Constable and
Maestro in *Missing* and *Crossing.*

For Birmingham Repertory Theatre he was
Curley in *Of Mice and Men*, Gideon in
Playland and Boaz in *Nativity.*

Elsewhere John has been Phil (and Jilll)
in *Phil and Jill and Jill and Phil* (Coventry
Belgrade and Worcester Swan); Angus in
Neville's Island ; Luther in *The Daughter In
Law,* and The Wizard in *The Wizard of Oz*
(Bolton Octagon); *The Winter's Tale* (Salisbury
Playhouse); *Don Juan* (West Yorkshire
Playhouse); *Happy Jack* and *Lucky Sods*
(Coliseum, Oldham); *A Midsummer Night's
Dream* (Dukes, Lancaster); *Mickey and Me*
and *Second from Last in the Sack Race*
(The Swan, Worcester).

On television John has worked on *Dalziel and
Pascoe, Cold Feet, The League of
Gentlemen, Emmerdale, Heartbeat, The Last
Train* and *The Butterfly Collector.*

He played Houdini in *Are You There Houdini*
for BBC World Service and read poetry by
Eleanor Cooke and Brian Patten for BBC
Radio 4's *Kaleidoscope.*

Anthony Clark
Director

Anthony started his career in 1981 as Arts
Council Assistant Director at The Orange
Tree Theatre, directing everything from a
school's tour of *Macbeth* to Martin Crimp's
first play *Living Remains*. In 1983, he joined
Tara Arts to direct their first two professional
productions, *Lion's Raj* and *Ancestral Voices*.
A year later he was appointed Artistic
Director of Contact Theatre in Manchester
where his productions included, *Romeo and
Juliet, Midsummer Night's Dream, The
Duchess of Malfi, Blood Wedding*
(Manchester Evening News Best Production
Award), *Mother Courage and her Children,
Oedipus, To Kill A Mockingbird* (Manchester
Evening News Best Production Award), *The
Power of Darkness* and new plays *Two
Wheeled Tricycle* by John Chambers, *Face
Value* by Cindy Artiste, *Green* by Tony Clark,
Homeland by Ken Blakeson and *McAlpine's
Fusiliers* by Kevin Fegan.

He joined Birmingham Repertory Theatre
Company in 1990 as Associate Director. His
many productions there include *Macbeth,
Julius Caesar, Aetheist's Tragedy* (TMA Best
Director Award), *The Seagull, Of Mice and
Men, Threepenny Opera, Saturday Sunday
Monday, The Grapes of Wrath, The Playboy
of the Western World, Pygmalion, St Joan,
The Entertainer* and David Lodge's *Home
Truths*. In 1997 he was appointed Associate
Artistic Director responsible for the launch
and programme of The Door (formerly
The Rep Studio), dedicated exclusively to
the promotion of new work. His recent
productions there include *Winnie The Witch,
Playing by The Rules* by Rod Dungate,
Nervous Women by Sara Woods, *Rough*
by Kate Dean, *Syme* (co-production with NT
Studio) by Michael Bourdages, *True Brit* by
Ken Blakeson, *Confidence* by Judy Upton,
Down Red Lane by Kate Dean, *Paddy
Irishmen* (co-production with the Tricycle
Theatre) by Declan Croghan, *All That Trouble*
by Paul Lucas, *Silence* (co-production with
Theatre Royal Plymouth) by Moira Buffini,
My Best Friend (co-production with
Hampstead Theatre) by Tamsin Oglesby,
Slight Witch (co-production with NT Studio)
by Paul Lucas and *Belonging* by Kaite
O'Reillly. He has freelanced extensively
including *Dr Faustus* (The Young Vic), *The
Red Balloon* (Bristol Old Vic and RNT – TMA
Best Show for Young People Award), *The
Snowman* (Leicester Haymarket), *Mother
Courage and Her Children* (RNT), *The Day
After Tomorrow* (RNT), *The Wood Demon*
(Playhouse) and *Loveplay* (RSC) by Moira
Buffini.

His writing credits include: *Hand it to Them*
(Orange Tree 1982), *Gone Egon* (Riverside
Studios 1983), *The Power of Darkness*
(Orange Tree 1983). *Wake* (Orange Tree
1984), *Tide Mark* (RSC 1984), *Green*
(Contact Theatre 1985), *Matter of Life and
Death* (National Theatre). His adaptations
for children which have been produced
throughout the country include: *The
Snowman, The Little Prince, The Red
Balloon, Pinocchio* and *Pied Piper*.
He has recently left The REP to pursue his
writing and freelance directing interests:
Tender by Abi Morgan (Hampstead Theatre
and Tour); *The Red Balloon* (BBC Radio 4);
Winnie the Witch (The Door, Birmingham
Repertory Theatre).

Biographies

Rachel Blues
Designer

Rachel trained at Edinburgh College of Art and Bristol Old Vic Theatre School.

For Birmingham Repertory Theatre: *Winnie the Witch, Belonging, Silence* (2000).

Recent designs include: *Top Girls* (Oxford Stage Company, West End and UK Tour 2002); *The Sleepers Den* (Southwark Playhouse); *Loveplay* (Royal Shakespeare Company: The Pit); *Ham* (New Vic Theatre, Stoke); *The Dove* (Warehouse Theatre Croydon); *Bouncers* (Octagon Theatre Bolton/Belgrade Theatre Coventry); *Car* (Theatre Absolute, Coventry Belgrade – winner of Fringe First); *Intimate Death* (Gate London). For the Coliseum Theatre, Oldham, *Rebecca, Brimstone and Treacle, Keeping Tom Nice, Lucky Sods, Second From Last in the Sack Race, Dead Funny, The Cemetery Club, Dancin' in the Street* and costumes for *Alfie – The Musical.* For the Swan Theatre Worcester, *Charley's Aunt, Private Lives* and *Elsie and Norm's Macbeth.*

In preparation: *Krindlekrax* (Birmingham Repertory Theatre, Nottingham Playhouse).

Production credit
Winspers Florists

THE REP

The Community Tour

Every year The REP takes a new play out on tour to community venues around Birmingham and the Midlands. This is the twenty-second Community Tour and to date The REP has performed to over 48,000 people.

The tour is an integral part of The Door's programme and a vital means of taking the work of the theatre into the community.

The Community Tour is **Supported by**

THE
SIR BARRY JACKSON
TRUST

Up Next in The Door . . .

Birmingham Repertory Theatre Company presents

No Sweat by Lloyd Withers

Thu 11 April – Sat 4 May

Chained to the production line in a car factory somewhere in the Midlands, Naz, Earl, Floyd, Devlin, Turbo, Doc and Zippy have got by until now – through backchat and banter, and supplementing their income with a few dodgy deals on the side. But when a foreign take-over looms, the gang are forced to question their own loyalties – and to discover just who their real mates are . . .

Lloyd Withers is from Birmingham and another writer developed by The REP's Attachment Scheme for writers. Brash, bold and funny, this is his debut play.

Paines Plough and Traverse Theatre Company present

Helmet by Douglas Maxwell

Tue 7 – Sat 11 May

Sal's selling up and getting out. Oldest son and biggest failure, his customers have long deserted him for brighter lights and newer releases. All except one. Enter Helmet in search of ultimate virtual thrill and escape, from the painful secret that made him who he is. Written by one of Scotland's most exciting and prolific young writers, *Helmet* is a funny, heartbreaking and hugely original play about 2 people struggling for happiness and dignity – trapped inside a computer game.

Birmingham Repertory Theatre Company presents

Getting to the Foot of the Mountain by Lisa Evans

Thu 16 May – Sat 8 June

"Some stories that are handed down are true. And some stories are just handed down."

When Danielle was a child, three women loomed large in her life: her gritty, responsible mother, her wild-child Aunt and their best friend. Now a young woman herself and facing the break-up of another relationship, Danielle takes stock of her childhood years – of an absent dad; of her fascination with neighbourhood "bad boy" - and, in so doing, uncovers a story of everyday heroism and the strange tricks that memory can play.

This is a warm and witty new play from the writer of the popular adaptations of the novels *East Lynne* and *The Tenant Of Wildfell Hall* for The REP's old Studio Theatre.

Moira Buffini
Silence

faber and faber

First published in 1999
by Faber and Faber Limited
3 Queen Square, London WC1N 3AU

Typeset by Country Setting, Kingsdown, Kent CT14 8ES
Printed in England by Intype London Ltd

A CIP record for this book
is available from the British Library

ISBN 0–571–20445–7

2 4 6 8 10 9 7 5 3 1

Characters

Ymma a lady
Agnés a servant
Eadric the king's man
Silence a youth
Roger a priest
Ethelred the king

Setting
Dark Age England

ACT ONE Canterbury
ACT TWO The Open Road
ACT THREE Cumbria

For my mother
Susan Buffini

Act One
Canterbury

ONE

A field in Kent.
  Ymma, a young noblewoman, is bent double in mid-vomit. Agnés, her servant, holds her hair. Eadric, a warrior, watches from a distance.

Agnés There we go. Get it all out. That's it.

Ymma Don't let them look at me.

Agnés (*to Eadric*) Show her some respect. She's the daughter of a saint!

  Eadric turns and walks away.

Ymma Pigs . . . (*Retches.*)

Agnés (*speaking out*) This is the fourth time since we left Normandy. The first was on the ship. We were approaching the English cliffs, gazing at the white land of our future. I was feeling almost hopeful, but Ymma went very quiet and said:

Ymma This is the beginning of the end, Agnés. This is the Kingdom of – (*Retches.*)

Agnés When we landed, the king's men met us on the harbour and loaded our belongings on a cart; bag after bag full of clothes. All she said to them was:

Ymma Don't come near me.

Agnés And she threw up again, spattering someone's boots. It was mortifying. An hour or so later, she made us stop outside a church. I thought she meant to say an urgent prayer to her sainted mother, but when I followed her in, I found she'd done a vomit in the font. I thought it blasphemous and I told her so.

Ymma Empty. Everything's out. There's only bile left . . .

Agnés You've got it in your hair.

Ymma I don't care.

Agnés You can't meet the king with vomit in your hair. Here. (*Agnés wipes her up.*) This is awful. You'll just have to tell him you're not used to English food.

Ymma Leave me!

Agnés Ymma, we have to get to Canterbury before nightfall. The men have been telling me about the raids they get after dark; Vikings, coming up the rivers like angels of death . . . We're late – it took me ages to clean up that font – and I'm scared.

Ymma I'm staying here.

Agnés You can't!

Ymma Why not? It makes no difference where I die.

Agnés Ymma, this is a new start in a new land –

Ymma It's a punishment, the whole damn thing. I'm here to be buried alive!

Agnés Your brother could have shut you away, locked you in an abbey for the mad! – But he's given you this wonderful chance. The English king's deciding your fate –

Ymma It's a trap!

Agnés It's whatever you make it! It all depends on how you behave. And look at you . . . Ymma, what about *me*? If you mess this up, what happens to me? It's so unfair!

Ymma (*stands*) I'm going to walk.

Agnés To Canterbury? You can't.

Ymma If this is my fate, Agnés, I'm going to meet it on foot, with my eyes wide open.

Agnés What about those men?

Ymma Make them follow me, fifty yards behind. They've been undressing me in their pigshit minds since we landed at Dover, and I don't want them close enough to hear my thoughts. If they question my behaviour, you can tell them I'm having a vision.

Agnés *What?*

Ymma I'm the daughter of a saint. Tell them I'm in an ecstasy of the spirit and that the Holy Virgin is at my side, leading me to my fate.

Agnés That's blasphemous!

Ymma It's not blasphemous, it's a beautiful lie. If you make it enchanting enough, they'll believe it.

Agnés Right. I'll tell them she's barefoot, immaculate, veiled in blue – whatever you like – and don't blame me if we get struck down!

Agnés exits. Ymma slowly surveys the landscape

Ymma Kent. What a dump.

TWO

A chapel.
    Water dripping. Silence, an adolescent lord, is before the altar, kneeling in a strange, un-Christian way. Roger enters, a youthful priest. He watches puzzled, disturbed.

Roger Lord Silence? I am a priest. My name is Roger. The bishops have sent me to find you. I – I've been selected from all God's servants in this holy place – on account of my youth and my mild and humble nature – to tell you of your fate, which the king himself has decided. I congratulate you, my lord. You're to be married to a French princess, Ymma of Normandy. It's my task to prepare you for that Blessed Sacrament.

Silence Pardon?

Roger The king, in his wisdom, is giving you a wife.

Silence Why?

Roger He has seen fit to decide your fate.

Silence What right has the king to decide my fate?

Roger He has divine right. He is a king.

Silence I'm puzzled, Sir. I have been puzzled since the moment I arrived and now I'm utterly confused. Does the king think me a fool?

Roger My lord,

Silence He sent envoys up to Cumbria, requesting my assistance. When I arrived, after an arduous journey, I was taken to his bedchamber and he said:

Ethelred (*from his bed, his face averted*) You have to help. My coasts are plagued with Viking raids and my people torment me with demands for protection. I hear you are of Viking blood. You know Viking language, Viking culture; you have an insight into the Viking mind. I want you to work with my men, to guide them, that they may better understand this demon race and purge it from our shores.

Silence I said Sire, I am honoured. The Vikings of course are not a demon race but I agree they must be stopped. They're even raiding up in Cumbria, where their own people have lived for generations. Majesty, our feelings are the same.

Ethelred has sat up, his crown askew: a naked,
scrawny youth. He is gazing at Silence.

Ethelred (*aghast*) What are you?

Silence I am Silence, Lord of Cumbria.

Ethelred This is impossible . . . The Lord of Cumbria is
a warrior!

Silence So I am.

Ethelred You're a LITTLE BOY!

Silence (*with dignity*) I'm fourteen.

Ethelred Are you telling me it was you who raised the
siege of York?

Silence That was my father. He is dead.

Ethelred I have been made a fool of! Madness and
chaos . . . Who brought this infant here? I'll have them
blinded!

Silence And his men pulled me out. No wonder the
Vikings are raiding this land. If I ruled Cumbria that
way –

Roger My lord, you cannot question the quality of
a king.

Silence My priest says that one should question
everything.

Roger To question a king is treason.

Silence She says that ignorance is our greatest enemy
and that only by questioning can we defeat it.

Roger She?

Silence A king who keeps his subjects in ignorance can
only be a tyrant!

Roger Your priest is a woman?

Silence Yes. Her name is Surr.

Roger My Lord, I –

Silence (*going to the altar.*) I'm going to light a candle. It's for my father. In times of trouble, I ask his advice.

Roger He is with Christ, my son.

Silence I'm glad. It's good to hear that Christ is in Valhalla.

Roger Uhh!

Silence It's a place of perpetual light.

Roger (*appalled*) Jesus Christ is *not* in Valhalla!

Silence (*lighting a candle*) You said he was with my father.

Roger But –

Silence My father is in Valhalla; if Christ is with him, he must be in Valhalla too.

Roger No, Valhalla / is a heathen myth –

Silence / And now I'll make sacrifice.

Roger What?

Silence Where do you keep your lambs?

Roger Are you intending . . . to slaughter a lamb on this altar?

Silence Of course. My priest says that when the way before you is shrouded in mist, the future is written in entrails. Priest . . . have I said something wrong?

   Roger faints.

THREE

The King's chamber.
  Ethelred is under his blankets. Eadric kneels by his bed.

Eadric And as we watched . . . Sire, there appeared a light beside her, and within it, slowly taking shape, was a lady veiled in blue. She was barefoot, immaculate, with her hands in an aspect of blessing. I wanted to drop to my knees but I didn't. I held back.

Ethelred (*appearing from out of the blankets*) What?

Eadric I held back.

Ethelred You saw *what*?

Eadric A lady. She hovered, Sire, with shining raiment underneath . . . I'm not a religious man, you know this. I'm a soldier. The only time I've ever seen things like this is after eating woodland fungi – the kind that gives a feeling of euphoria in battle – and I haven't touched any, I swear it.

Ethelred Are you telling me you saw the Blessed Virgin walking with Ymma of Normandy?

Eadric I wouldn't like to say. But whoever it was, she didn't have no mud, even on the soles of her feet. Incandescent is a word I'd like to use. Radiant. Possibly diaphanous . . .

Ethelred Eadric, it was a trick of the setting sun.

Eadric I saw it.

Ethelred It was her shadow or something.

Eadric It communicated with my mind. Sent me thoughts so beautiful I wept. I feel changed.

Ethelred Eadric, you are my strength of arm, my executioner, chief architect of all my violent acts. Please believe me when I say this is rubbish.

Eadric Sire, lies do not come from the mouth of Eadric Longshaft. I saw a shining vision!

Ethelred Very well, you saw a vision. It spoke to your mind. Who am I to argue? Only the king. (*Pause.*) I've decreed the lady's fate. She's marrying Silence of Cumbria.

Eadric I beg you, Sire; meet her before you decide.

Ethelred Her brother sent her here for punishment, and puishment she'll get. Cumbria is a wasteland on the edge of the civilised world and its lord is a juvenile fool.

Eadric But what if she is holy? I saw her walk in Godlight!

Ethelred Too late. The proclamation's already been read.

Eadric She is so other-worldly, Sire, that she cannot keep down her food!

Ethelred Well, what can I do? I won't go back on it. I can't change my mind, can I? CAN I!

Eadric No, Sire.

Ethelred You know what they whisper behind my back! Feeble, vacillating, vague . . . Do you think I like it? It *pains* me. Oh God, all this trouble! If you're so taken with her, Eadric, make her your responsibility, not mine. When she's wed, you can escort her up to the icy North and play with visions all the way. Oh, I am exhausted in my labours for this land, worn out with my exertions and no one, no one cares. Eadric, have pity. If you're human, have pity on your king . . .

Eadric looks at the king, without pity.

FOUR

The chapel.

Water dripping. Roger approaches Silence, zealously excited.

Roger Lord Silence, since we spoke, I've been seeking the help of God. I threw myself down in my cell and said, 'God, what am I to do? Lord Silence is a heathen, a worshipper of fiends –'

Silence Pardon?

Roger '– but when I look at him, I see no evil in his face; he is but a youth who's been led astray.'

Silence I don't worship fiends!

Roger 'How may I, Roger, who has crept out his youth in sandals, meek in the shadow of crypts and cloisters, how may I save him from damnation?' At that moment, I saw a great flurry of leaves swirl away in the wind towards the North and I knew that God was sending me a sign. He was saying, 'Roger, take this boy. Fill him with my Word. Go with him to Cumbria and educate him in my ways.'

Silence I have a God: Odin. I see no need to learn about yours.

Roger Lord Silence, your heathen faith endangers you most terribly. Please hear me. If they find it out, they will slaughter you. You must discover God.

Silence So you wish to teach me – to keep me safe?

Roger Yes! Safe in his hand forever more. I prayed that my days would not end in the library, crumbling in parchments, and now my prayers have come true. Please, let me take you by the hand and lead your spirit into grace.

Silence (*moved*) Are you saying . . . that you wish to be my friend?

Roger Your friend, yes. Your guide, your brother.

Silence I have no friends here. I am alone.

Roger Alone, no longer. You have me. (*Embraces Silence.*) And the Lord!

Eadric enters, with Ymma and Agnés.

Eadric (*indicating Silence*) The Lord of Cumbria.

Roger Women! My God, it must be her. Quick, kneel, pray – do something!

Ymma There must be some mistake.

Roger Lady of Normandy and . . . other gracious lady, please accept a welcome from God's humblest servant in this place. I am a priest. My name is Roger. I offer up a prayer of thanks at your safe arrival –

Ymma Am I to marry you? Or the little boy?

Silence Lady, I am Silence, Lord of Cumbria. My borders stretch from Lancaster to the land of Strathclyde. I come at the king's own request from Ragnarok, my castle in the North. It's his will we should be wed and there's nothing we can do. So hello.

Ymma I'm to marry your father, surely.

Silence My father's dead.

Agnés (*pause. To Ymma*) He'll grow, my lady.

Ymma Agnés, I had imagined cruelty. What I've got is ridicule. It's worse . . . I'm to be married to a child.

Silence I've been ruling Cumbria since I was born. No one there would dare to call me child.

Roger Gracious lady, noble lord, this marriage is wished by our royal king –

Ymma Then curse him! *Curse* him! (*She exits.*)

Agnés My lady's unwell. The rigours of the journey; English food –

Ymma (*re-enters*) Tell me, Priest, how are we to consummate it? He's a baby! (*Re-exits.*)

Agnés I'm sorry; please don't judge her, or me. We're not like this. (*She exits.*)

Roger She spoke of consummation; I feel faint. Why did she scorn you? People marry children all the time.

Silence I'm fourteen! I'm not a child!

Roger No, no, no, of course not! . . . But my lord, her objections shouldn't be taken to heart. I've done much reading on the subject of women and I know their characters well, though my experience of them is scant. They are weak, capricious creatures –

Silence She doesn't want to marry me –

Roger Nonsense –

Silence And I don't want to marry her!

Roger My Lord, have pity!

Silence Pity?

Roger She cannot help herself. Women are foolish. It tells us so in our Holy Books. The soul of a woman is an inferior thing, a dark shadow, compared to the brilliant soul of a man. It's made of tarnished metal, a weak and rusting substance that must be constantly polished by a strong male hand. Women are naturally inclined to evil. They are created inferior, responsible for our fall and all our agonies on Earth. Now, Ymma of Normandy is a woman alone. She has no male hand to guide her, no one to save her from herself. Think of the peril she is in. If you don't wed her, who will bring her meagre soul closer to God?

Eadric looks heavenwards, closing his eyes.

FIVE

The King's chamber.
Ymma enters in a rage. She is trying to get her dress off, clawing at the back. Ethelred appears from his blankets and watches her, amazed.

Ymma Damn you! *Bastards*! Damn my damn brother! Damn this nation of Saxon pigs and their bastard, BASTARD KING! They will not break me! I'll NOT BREAK! Hate. Hate this dress, hate it!

Ethelred Good evening.

Ymma (*turning, shocked*) What are you doing? This is MY CHAMBER!

Ethelred No, it's –

Ymma Get OUT! Agnés, AGNÉS! . . .

Ethelred This is *my* chamber. I am Ethelred, your bastard, bastard king.

Ymma laughs incredulously. Ethelred puts on his crown. Pause. Ymma kneels.

Ymma Your Majesty. I'm lost –

Ethelred I don't recall ordering a whore this evening.

Ymma I am Ymma of Normandy, Sire.

Ethelred You come into my bedchamber with a mouthful of curses and you start to take off your clothes. What am I to think?

Ymma I thought this was my chamber.

Ethelred You can only be a whore.

Ymma I thought I was alone. In private!

Ethelred So in private you think the king's a bastard and you curse his name? Continue. You were undressing.

Ymma I . . .

Ethelred Please carry on. Don't let me interrupt you. Do you require payment first? I never pay first. To speak truthfully, I never pay at all. That is my prerogative as king; and if a whore displeases me, I have her killed. Undress.

Ymma When I saw the white cliffs of this land, I should have thrown myself from the boat rather than set one foot on it. I could have been at peace by now, lying free, inviolate, under the weight of the great sea.

Ethelred May I remind you that to disobey a king is treason, punished by death.

Ymma (*turning on him*) I would rather be dead than standing here! So, bastard, why don't you kill me? KILL ME!

Ethelred is speechless.

Is this how you live? I hear you never leave your bed. It stinks in here, like a foetid prison. Are you a prisoner, Your Majesty?

Ethelred What do you mean?

Ymma You look as if you've never had a moment's freedom in your life.

Ethelred Like all true monarchs I am slave to my subjects. And I serve them best by being here, in my bed.

Ymma So you lie there scratching while the Vikings ravage your land?

Ethelred I am engaged in a battle – a grave battle!

Ymma With fleas and bedbugs?

Ethelred With God!

Ymma Oh, with God . . .

Ethelred I am trying to save my England from destruction. I can only do this by discovering God's will. He is angry and I, his instrument on earth, must appease him. There is no greater work I could do.

Ymma You're afraid, aren't you?

Ethelred To be afraid of God is a virtue.

Ymma But you're afraid of everything. The most powerful man in England and you're shaking with fear.

Ethelred Your brother said, in his letter, that you were dangerous. He said you had all the malice and cunning of the viciously insane.

Ymma Then why don't you kill me?

Ethelred What did you do, for him to cast you out? He's put the mark of Cain on you. What crime did you commit?

Ymma My brother is a snake, but he's a powerful snake. You're just a snake. Look at you.

Ethelred Eadric! EADRIC!

Eadric enters.

Ethelred This is a whore. It has offended me.

Eadric Sire –

Ethelred Take her away. Watch until she is wed. See she doesn't harm herself.

Ymma You coward.

Ethelred You've been sent to me for punishment and you'll live to savour every moment of your fate!

Eadric escorts Ymma out. Ethelred rocks in his blankets.

I am *not* afraid . . .

SIX

The chapel.
   Water dripping. Silence and Roger.

Roger . . . So that is the story of our Lord, Jesus Christ. I'll fill in the details later but all you need to know is that he died to take away our sins. Which brings me to confession. Tomorrow you must stand pure before God and in order to be pure, you must be confessed. It is time, my son, to clean your soul. I'll discuss the dark cornucopia of human sins and vices in due course but as we're so pressed for time we must begin with sins of the flesh.

Silence Sins of the flesh?

Roger The most insidious sins of all. What else can reduce a man to the behaviour of a beast? Silence, you must know that even if you have not sinned with your body, you may have sinned in your thoughts. All thoughts which linger on the flesh, are sinful. Even our dreams can sin.

Silence I'd like to confess my puzzlement. I'm extremely puzzled, Sir.

Roger You must call me Father.

Silence On the journey from Cumbria, Father, the king's envoys were telling me of fucking.

Roger That is a sinful word! The word you need is . . . consummation: the Sacred Act.

Silence Sacred Act . . . They told me how the Thing between my legs will grow out of nothing.

Roger Ah, Thing, yes –

Silence That it will make me into a man, from a boy, into a man and never go back – And I'm worried. Really frankly extremely puzzled and worried.

Roger Silence. This is not exactly a confession –

Silence Yes, but I'm not worried about sin, I'm worried that it won't happen with me.

Roger That what won't happen?

Silence The Thing won't grow.

Roger Ah . . . Has the Thing never grown of its own accord? . . . Perhaps as the result of a dream, a devilish planting of desire in the mind during sleep? Or perhaps as the result of accidentally brushing against the flesh of another?

Silence My priest told me that some men had Things and some men didn't.

Roger My son, all men have Things! Your heathen priest is an ignorant woman. Disregard all she says! You have a Thing and the Thing will grow. It's a natural phenomenon. You'll become familiar with it in time and really, the feeling is quite . . . innocuous.

Silence Has it ever happened to you?

Roger Occasionally . . . I am able to subdue it with the power of prayer. Silence, you must have had some experience of your Thing?

Silence I once had a dream where – (*Pause.*)

Roger Where what? I am your confessor, Silence, and you must tell me all. It may have been an evil dream and we need to find out so that you can repent and I can absolve you. That is how confession works.

Silence I was in the forest. It was winter light, coming horizontal through the trees, and there was snow lying heavy on the ground. I was naked.

Roger Ah.

Silence But the strange thing is that I felt no cold, just a kind of . . .

Roger An excitement of the flesh?

Silence Yes. My nerves were all on end. I felt completely alive. I was hunting. Only, it wasn't an animal I was hunting. It was a man.

Roger A man?

Silence With dark hair and arms like Odin himself.

Roger Oh.

Silence He hid in the trees ahead – and he came at me out of nowhere! I leapt on him and fought – and he drew me close to him. I thought he was going to kill me but –

Roger But what?

Silence He kissed me.

Roger Ah.

Silence And everything went peculiar. I was pulling his hair and kicking, but he held me closer and closer and I could feel my legs go limp so I grappled and yelled, 'I'll fight you to the end you –'

Roger Barbarian, yes!

Silence And he threw me to the ground and my lips went on his and we . . . There came a feeling, here . . . Like flying! My senses soared – all six of them at once! – and I awoke.

Roger And upon waking . . . was your Thing not large?

Silence No sir.

Roger There had been no expulsion of liquid?

Silence Um. There was some moisture, yes.

Roger Ah. This moisture. Did you know what it was?

Silence No, Sir.

Roger It was the seed of life. A man puts this seed into the woman, with his Thing, during The Act. You shall put it into your wife and create an heir for Cumbria. Do you understand? (*Silence nods.*) You must not think of the barbarian in the forest. It was an evil dream, doubly evil because . . . he was a man. Now, do you repent of it?

Silence Yes, Sir.

Roger You must call me Father. I absolve you, in the name of the Father, the Son and the Holy Spirit, Amen. You can pray, if you like, for your Thing. You must ask God to make it large only when it is fitting; that is with your wife, in the marriage bed, preferably not more than twice a week and never on a Holy Day. (*Adjusts his crotch in embarrassed discomfort.*) You must go now.

Silence Why?

Roger Our lesson on sin is over. I am overcome with a desire to pray privately. Please go.

Silence Is it something I've said?

Roger No. I'm just asking you to leave!

Silence (*watching him*) . . . It's your Thing, isn't it?

Roger Silence, do not shame me!

Silence . . . The Thing is shameful then?

Roger Yes! Yes!!

Silence leaves, puzzled and upset.

Power of prayer: God calm me . . . Bishops. I must think of bishops, dead fish and bishops, bishops, bishops . . .

SEVEN

A large chamber.
Ymma is wearing a wedding gown. Agnés is pinning on her veil. Eadric watches.

Agnés The king's had a dozen nuns working through the night to finish this on time. I heard they almost went blind, huddling round candles. You look wonderful. Good luck, Ymma. My heart is with you, on this, your wedding day. (*Pause.*) Well, thank you Agnés. You've made me look lovely; what skill you have. Oh, that's all right; it's the pinnacle of a lady's lady's career, dressing her lady for her nuptial feast.

Ymma Are we to have this *thing* here all day?

Eadric I'm under orders. I must watch.

Ymma And what about my wedding night? Will you stay and watch that too, dog?

23

Agnés Forgive my lady; she's overwrought – girlishly excited. (*to Ymma*) Please! This is our last chance. I beg you, just accept it.

Ymma Agnés, shut up, or I will scream like a maniac until they lock me away.

Agnés Pinnacle of my career and this is it. (*Picks up two posies. Hands one to Ymma*) Here. Try not to wilt them.

The wedding: music. Silence stands beside Ymma, who is staring straight ahead. Eadric watches; Ethelred observes. Roger, conducting the service, is extremely nervous.

Roger And the Lord God caused a deep sleep to fall on Adam and He took one of his ribs and closed up the flesh thereof: And the rib, which the Lord God had taken from man, made He into a woman (*joining their hands*) and brought her unto the man. And Adam said:

Silence (*as a vow*) This is now bone of my bones, and flesh of my flesh.

Ymma (*in reply*) She shall be called woman.

Roger Because she was taken out of man. Therefore shall a man leave his father and mother and cleave unto his wife: and they shall be one flesh.

Silence tries to kiss Ymma. Can't reach. Roger blesses them.

And they were both naked, the man and his wife, and were not ashamed.

Ethelred Amen!

Ethelred leaves. Roger and Agnés bring forward a bed. They leave. Eadric backs out, his eyes still on Ymma. Silence and Ymma are alone. The moment grows agonising.

Silence I like your dress. (*Gently touches it.*)

Ymma (*flinching*) What are you doing?

Silence I wanted to touch it.

Ymma Well. I'm your wife. I suppose you can touch anything.

> *Ymma holds out her arm. Silence touches the fabric.*

Why are you called Silence?

Silence My mother chose it. I was born just after my father died. They say she was depressed.

> *Ymma removes her arm.*

Your mother was a saint, wasn't she?

Ymma So they say.

Silence Did she have a halo?

Ymma A what?

Silence A crown of celestial light. The pictures in the church have them. The Priest told me what they were. I thought they were hats.

Ymma No. My mother didn't have a halo.

Silence Then how did people know she was a saint?

Ymma They made her a saint after she was dead.

Silence So . . . during her life, she was just ordinary?

Ymma Yes.

Silence I thought saints had powers, like gods.

Ymma Only after they're dead. Their remains have power.

Silence What like?

Ymma I don't know – healing, casting out spirits, whatever.

Silence Can your mother do that?

Ymma If you don't mind, I'd rather not talk about her.

Silence Why not?

Ymma Because your questions are childish.

Silence You shouldn't speak to me like that.

Ymma How should I speak to you?

Silence With respect.

Ymma (*she turns her back*) Undo this, would you? It's so tight it's making me sick.

Silence I'll call your maid.

Ymma No, I don't want her in here. You do it. (*Pause.*) My Lord.

Silence gets under the veil and starts to clumsily undo the gown.

Silence I don't think you should judge me on account of my age. It's an accident of birth, not something I can help. I'm willing to try and if you were too, we'd . . . (*Laughs, playing with the veil.*) This is so clean; like being lost in mist. It's like snow! . . .

Ymma Tell me about Cumbria. If I'm to live there, I should know the worst. I've heard that people share their beds with pigs and drag their knuckles on the ground.

Silence (*hurt. Pulls roughly at the back of the dress*) I can't do this. Do it yourself.

Silence moves away, caught up it the veil. Fights with it. Manages to get it off. Ymma tries to undo the back

of her gown. She can't. It's like a straitjacket. She
reaches the point of tears.

Silence I'm sorry, let –

Ymma Agnés, AGNÉS!

Agnés (*enters.*) What?

Ymma Get me out of this. Those nuns have sewn their misery into every seam.

Agnés Right. (*to Silence*) Oh dear. Nervous fingers . . .

Ymma My husband was about to tell me of Cumbria, that vast bogland in the freezing North, where fate has flung us.

Silence From the minute I met you, you've been rude to me. You know nothing about me, or my home!

Ymma And I'm wedded to it for the rest of my life!

Silence turns away.

Agnés (*to Ymma*) Look at him. He's trying not to cry.

Ymma So what?

Agnés He's a little boy . . . You could have had some brute who'd have raped you twice by now and beaten you for crying. If I were you I'd count my blessings.

Ymma Well, you're not me, are you?

Silence Cumbria is beautiful. It's a land of green mountains and still waters, of forests and cold rivers and I only have to think of it to know that I am strong. My priest says Ragnarok, my home, was there before the Romans came. For a thousand years people have lived within its walls – and now it's ours. We're a new people, a bold people – Viking and British – and we love our land. But the land is wild. I am lord only of the

27

people, not of the land. The land is free. That is Cumbria, lady. More beautiful than you deserve.

Ymma (*pause*) Thank you, Agnés. You may leave.

Agnés I'll just turn the bed down.

Ymma I said go.

Agnés goes.

I'm spiteful and cruel. I carry rage around in my heart. I've never earned anyone's love. I'm vicious and vengeful and even my servants despise me. I'll make you a terrible wife.

Silence You remind me of my priest.

Ymma What?

Silence She's holding the reins of my government while I'm away. She's powerful like you, but she isn't angry.

Ymma Your priest is a woman?

Silence Yes. Why are you so angry?

Ymma It's my nature . . . (*She sighs.*) I should have been a man. My anger would have been a virtue then. But I'm not a man. I'm this.

Ymma takes off her dress and stands in her shift. She throws the dress to Silence. Pause. Silence carries it to a chair, and lays it down as if it were a dying person.

Silence So. Consummation . . .

Ymma Yes.

Silence The Sacred Act.

Ymma Sacred? Is that what they told you? (*a slight, contemptuous laugh*) Well, come on then. (*She sits on the bed.*) Forgive me, but the sooner we . . . achieve it, the sooner we can go to sleep. It's been a long day.

Silence Some other time, I think.

Ymma Pardon?

Silence Out of consideration for your unpolished soul, I've decided to defer it.

Ymma Lord Silence, they'll check the sheets in the morning.

Silence What for?

Ymma To make sure we've sealed our fate. If the marriage isn't consummated, it's worthless. Didn't they tell you that? It's a bond of blood.

Silence Blood? . . .

Ymma (*pause*) Won't you look at me? (*Sighs.*) Oh you poor little boy –

Silence Get into bed and shut your mouth! I am not poor! I am not little! I am NOT a BOY! I'm a MAN!

Ymma (*getting into bed*) Right. Please yourself. (*She pulls the covers over her head.*)

Silence I'm saying my prayers . . . And then you'd better watch out! (*Prays.*) Dear Lord, bring happiness to my union. Now. (*Checks to see if anything is growing.*) Now! I need it NOW, GOD! (*Fumbles. Panics. Kneels in an un-Christian way.*) Odin, help. With your power, make me a man. Please. PLEASE! . . .

Silence approaches the bed. Jumps on Ymma and clumsily kisses her, groping her breasts. Ymma can't breathe. Eventually she shoves Silence off.

Ymma God Almighty.

Silence (*distraught*) It won't / happen!

Ymma / You could have warned me.

Silence I can't do it! It won't grow.

Ymma What are you talking about?

Silence My Thing!

Ymma Of course it'll grow. You're nervous, that's all . . .

Silence No! I saw the envoys pee and I can't do it like that.

Ymma Don't be stupid.

Silence (*sobs*) I don't know where it is!

Ymma Oh for Heaven's sake! . . . Here.

Silence Don't touch me!

Ymma Silence, I can grow it for you.

Silence NO!

Ymma Pull yourself together – (*struggling*) – this is difficult enough as it is.

Silence Get off!

Ymma Come here! (*Tears open Silence's trousers.*) I'll sort your Thing out!

Silence Leave me, witch! I said GET OFF!

Ymma Don't be such a baby! (*hand in trousers*) What's . . .? Oh my God, you haven't got one!

Silence wails.

You're a girl . . .

Silence WHAT?

Ymma You're a girl!

Silence UHH!

Ymma Mother of God . . . I married a girl.

30

Silence I'm a BOY! I'm my mother's son, Lord of Cumbria!

Ymma Silence – *(feeling under her clothes)* you've got breasts.

Silence No –

Ymma And look – boys have bollocks – where are yours?

Silence NO! –

Ymma You're a girl!

Silence God HELP ME!

Ymma . . . Don't tell me you didn't know.

Silence I'm Lord Silence of Cumbria! Lord Silence! A man!

Ymma Look at us . . . We're both the same.

Silence looks. She buries her head in the bedclothes and whimpers.

This is incredible. How have you lived your whole life not knowing what you are?

Silence I'm a boy, a boy. They said I was a boy.

Ymma Why would they do that? They've turned you against your own nature!

Silence Jesus protect me. Odin protect me.

Ymma What if my mother had done it to me? Oh my God, I'd be Duke of Normandy! . . .

Silence Don't let me be female. Women have shrunken souls . . .

Ymma Do you see what your mother's done? She's given you power, freedom and power! You're a lord. As a woman you'd have lost everything; as a man, you have it all!

Silence (*helplessly*) What will I do? . . .

Ymma A little girl. (*She laughs.*)

Silence Don't laugh

Ymma The king of England has married me to a little girl.

Silence Don't you dare! (*She pins Ymma down.*) I will kill you if you laugh! I mean it.

Ymma Do you know what our marriage is, Lady Silence? It's a sacrilege. Solemnly, in front of God, that priest has joined two women in wedlock. Do you know what the Bible says about that?

Silence No.

Ymma Abomination. You've deceived the king. Do you know what he'll do to you when he finds out?

Silence Send me home?

Ymma Silence, he'll put your head on a pole. Nothing will be punishment enough.

Silence Why didn't Surr tell me? And my mother . . . How *could* they? Abomination; what will I do?

Ymma I don't know. It's a shame you're not pretty. Pretty women can be so moving when they plead . . .

Silence When will you tell them? Will you wait until morning or do you want to do it now?

Ymma Agnés, AGNÉS!

Silence Yes, yes, get it over. Do it now. Let me die.

Agnés enters in her night attire, carrying a candle.

Agnés What?

Silence Forgive me!

Agnés That's all right, my lord. I'm used to being called out of bed at the most horrendous hours to indulge Ymma's whims.

Ymma My husband, Lord Silence of Cumbria is . . . thirsty. He'd like some wine.

Silence looks at her in amazement.

Agnés Right. Wine.

Ymma Can you imagine? He tells me he's never tasted French wine.

Agnés Oh, my lord hasn't lived.

Ymma No. But he's going to start living now. I've been telling him, Agnés, French wine is like poetry. It's known as the drink of love, and of freedom and truth. We should toast our union with it. We've made a vow to be flesh and bone together. We should love and protect each other, don't you think?

Silence Yes . . . Bring us wine, thank you.

Agnés Well, I'm delighted. Oh, I could cry. I thought she'd break your arms, my lord.

Ymma Out!

Agnés Congratulations, you're truly a man now. (*She leaves.*)

Silence (*embraces Ymma.*) Thank you. Thank you.

Ymma You strange creature. Strange, strange creature. Silence . . .

Silence (*they part*) A woman's wisdom lies in her silence.

Ymma What?

Silence My mother used to say it, when I was a b –
a child. I never understood it before. Your face is so
perfect it frightens me. Your clothes amaze me. I can't be
the same as you; you're beautiful.

Ymma Silence, are you aware of what I've just done?

Silence You've saved my life. My bride is beautiful and
she's saved my life.

Ymma If they find out what you are, they'll have my
head. It would be difficult trying to function without it.

Silence Yes.

Ymma So we must learn to lie.

Silence No, why should we lie? We need only stay silent.
You can hide anything in a silence. (*Pause.*) What'll we
do about the sheets? We have to seal our fate.

Ymma Blood and spit. Give me your knife and I'll cut
myself.

Silence No. Let me.

Ymma To tell you the truth, I was going to have to do
something about them anyway.

Silence Why?

Ymma Oh . . . I'm not a virgin.

Silence (*speaking out*) Later that night, as the dawn in
the window gave us every shade of brilliant blue, my
wife and I enjoyed a jug of ruby wine and watched the
room slowly saturate with colour. Why had she called
herself spiteful and cruel? She was warmth and laughter
unfolding before my eyes. We promised over our bond
of blood, that neither of us would ever reveal my true
identity. She said the truth was a jewel to be hidden.

As the first beams of sunlight began to fill the room with gold, we began to plan our lives in Cumbria. She said we should allow each other freedom in all things and our freedom would cleave us together. It seemed impossible that we were a sacrilege and impossible that I was the same creature as my strange and beautiful spouse. I thanked the gods, abomination though I was, for bringing me to her, and making her my wife.

EIGHT

A courtyard.
   Ethelred is huddled in blankets, rocking in distress. He wears his crown but little else.

Ethelred (*looking skywards*) Is it God I wrestle with, or the devil? Why do you play with me? What does it MEAN?

   Roger enters, dressed for travelling. He is shocked by Ethelred's appearance.

Roger Your Majesty? . . . I am a Priest. My name is Roger.

Ethelred Priest,

Roger Forgive me, but you seem . . . Perhaps you have some clothing or some footwear I could bring?

Ethelred I'm troubled by a dream. I wish to know if it has power.

Roger Um, dreams are not my area of expertise, Majesty. I'm more of a parchment man –

Ethelred I dreamt last night of the end of the world.

Roger The end of the world?

Ethelred The apocalypse. It's made a wreck of me! Priest, I must have the meaning.

Roger Sire, permit me to find you a bishop, or a more senior –

Ethelred No, you, now! I awoke – in my dream – to find that the ground was shaking. Like this – all shaking! I came out here, where we are now, and there was a rumbling and people wailing in distress, women, old men, pathetic people of all kinds. I thought 'bastards' and I raised my hand to bless them. Then it came. There was a roar. Masonry shattered and the land cracked open.

Roger Goodness.

Ethelred Flames went as high as the moon.

Roger What did you do?

Ethelred Screamed. I screamed and screamed.

Roger Ah.

Ethelred In horrible silence, as one does in dreams. It was the apocalypse, Priest.

    Eadric enters, laden with weapons. He listens.

Roger I've – I've had similar dreams myself . . . Perhaps they are the inevitable fear of our times, living as we do on the edge of destruction.

Ethelred You believe we're on the edge of destruction?

Roger Oh yes. There are signs and portents all around us – the Vikings, for example. My theological brothers believe that they are the last enemies of the righteous, and that the end is very close.

Ethelred Priest, do you think my dream could be a portent of the end?

Roger Well . . .

Ethelred Because there's more.

Roger Oh.

Ethelred There I was, screaming in the fire, but in the midst of God's carnage, in the very eye of the last catastrophe, I was untouched. Others were consumed all around but I was unburning, unbloody! And then, I saw her . . .

Roger Who?

Ethelred Ymma of Normandy.

Roger Ah.

Ethelred There, at the crux of the dream. She was crawling towards me, her clothes all torn, covered in dirt and grime, her thighs grazed, breasts heaving –

Roger Heavens above.

Ethelred And in her face, was . . .

Roger Was what?

Ethelred (*moved*) Love.

Roger She is the daughter of a saint.

Ethelred She grasped me. I gave a small cry, a kind of 'aahhh . . . ' and fell into her arms. She was brimful of . . . deep depths. She clutched me.

Roger Ah.

Ethelred And then we kissed. It was like music in my mouth.

Roger Oh.

Ethelred We fornicated. In the flames.

Roger Uh.

Ethelred I think it was love, Priest. It was profound. And when we finished, all was quiet. We had survived. (*Pause.*) What do you make of it? Will it help me pray for salvation? To know that I've fucked my way through the apocalypse?

Roger Majesty, I can give you a penance for this dream.

Ethelred I'm not looking for a penance! I'm looking for the meaning.

Roger (*adjusting his crotch*) Perhaps it means you should pray. There is much to be said for the power of prayer.

Ethelred She walked through these gates with a Holy vision. She found her way to my room. God put her in my sight. She opened her heart to me, touched me with the truth, and I've married her to – (*suddenly realising*) I should have married her myself! Oh GOD! (*Flings himself down.*) Why didn't you *tell* me? Oh, you BASTARD! . . .

> *Eadric drops his weapons. He lifts Ethelred into his arms and roughly calms his tantrum, as if this is a duty he's done many times before, but doesn't relish. He looks accusingly at Roger.*

Roger I am a priest. My name is Roger. I – I was just passing, humbly on my way to meet the newly-weds. I'm to accompany them into the North.

Eadric Why?

Roger They will need guidance.

Eadric I'm the guide.

Roger Spiritual guidance, my friend. God's protection.

Eadric I'm the protector.

Roger Well, splendid . . . You and how many others? What kind of a retinue are we to have?

Eadric None.

Roger We have only one protector?

Eadric The fewer people who travel, the less chance of attack. I've disguised the cart as best I can, to resemble a peasant vehicle. We go unobtrusively. It's our best chance.

Roger It is perilous then?

Eadric The roads have never been worse. But it's my belief that the cart is blessed and will come to no harm.

Roger What makes you say that?

Eadric We travel with the daughter of a saint.

Silence (*enters*) Father, guess what? The sacred act was indeed sacred –

Roger My son, you're before the king.

Silence (*kneels*) I'd like to thank you Sire, for giving me my gorgeous and wonderful bride. May Odin reward you with a place in Valhalla! –

Ethelred *What*?

Silence In heaven! May Jesus Lord Christ God bless you and reward you, Amen.

Ethelred (*appalled*) Priest, he is a heathen!

Roger No longer, Sire! He received baptism just before he was wed. I intend him to become God's own vessel, a shining light of Jesus in the North!

Ethelred So, I have married the daughter of a saint to a godless Viking devil.

Ymma (*enters, with Agnés.*) Good morning, Sire

Ethelred Leave us, all of you, NOW! LEAVE US!

All exit except Ymma.

Don't look at me, I'm a mess. Avert your eyes. (*Ymma looks away.*) You can see the husband I've given you. He's a fool, a heathen savage! I've made you ridiculous.

Ymma Not at all.

Ethelred I wish to apologise. I had your fate in my hands and look what I did!

Ymma I'm happy with your choice.

Ethelred No! I wish to rectify the situation. It may not be too late.

Ymma Sire –

Ethelred Speak freely: did you consummate? If not, I can have it annulled. I can annul it and you can stay here, in court. You can forget the whole idea of going to Cumbria. I can send him packing and have you, Ymma, here, with me.

Ymma As your whore?

Ethelred No, NO! As my wife. As Queen, consecrated Queen of England.

Ymma . . . You would annul my marriage to Lord Silence and marry me yourself?

Ethelred Yes. With my unreserved apology.

Ymma Why?

Ethelred Ask not for a reason. Let it grow. Like a bloom . . . Ymma, you asked me for freedom. This is it: freedom and power.

Ymma I have knowledge of my husband.

Ethelred (*devastated*) Is that the truth?

Ymma My husband has knowledge of me.

Ethelred But think what I'm offering! Consecrated queen!

Ymma I'm sorry. It would offend God.

Ethelred No, no, God wishes it! Oh, I could kill myself for calling you a whore! What was I *thinking* of?

Ymma I belong to Silence of Cumbria with vows I cannot break!

Ethelred He's a pagan; the marriage is void! (*Grabs her.*) Ymma, I know where your feelings lie.

Ymma Get / – (*struggling*) NO!

Ethelred I've seen the love on your face. I've felt the passion of your kiss. / In my dreams –

Ymma Don't touch me! Get – DON'T TOUCH ME!

Ymma punches Ethelred in the face. He reels backwards and passes out. Pause.

Ymma What have I done? What have I done? (*Sinks to her knees.*) Oh God! . . . Every time a good thing comes, every time I think my life might shine, just for a moment –

She sees Eadric. She looks at him aghast. Silence enters.

Silence What happened?

Ymma I hit him. It's over. He'll come round and this dog will carry me away!

Eadric picks up Ethelred. He takes him to a corner. He drops him in a heap. He hurls the crown away. Ymma and Silence watch, flabbergasted.

Eadric Let's go.

Roger (*entering*) Where's his Majesty? I was going to ask him to bless our cart.

Eadric He's gone.

Ymma We're leaving. Now! We go by no main roads, we pass through no towns. We ask help from no one and we don't stop until we reach the North. We go like *fugitives*!

    Eadric bows. Ymma sweeps past him. Eadric exits, after her.

Silence Father, my wife is amazing.

Act Two
The Open Road

NINE

The cart.
  *Ymma, Roger and Agnés in the back, Eadric and
Silence in the front.*

Silence It was our second day in the cart.

Ymma For hours I looked over my shoulder, expecting
the king and all his men to descend upon us. But nothing
happened. No furies came.

Silence I was looking at our saviour, Eadric Longshaft,
trying to think who he reminded me of, when he said
something strange.

Eadric Dog.

  Ymma begins to sing. She has a high, eerie voice.

Silence Every time I look at you, Eadric, I think I've seen
you somewhere before. Did you know that?

Eadric No.

Silence My wife . . . I didn't know she could sing. I learn
something about her every day; like finding new jewels
in a box full of treasure. Are you married?

Eadric Was.

Silence What happened?

Eadric (*resents being asked*) She's dead.

Silence Oh . . . How did she – ?

Eadric Vikings took her. I found her spoiled.

43

Silence Spoiled?

Eadric So I killed her. Anything else?

Silence He didn't speak again for the rest of the day.

Roger (*speaking out*) The open land; we are exposed, dazed and wriggling, like beetles under a lifted stone. I cannot raise my eyes. When I try, my stomach lurches and my head spins. It makes me want to weep in shame. Why am I afraid? How is it possible for a man to be afraid of fields?

Agnés Father, are you cold?

Roger No, good lady.

Agnés You're shaking. I thought you might be –

Roger No no no. Not cold . . .

Agnés I was wondering if you'd hear my confession sometime.

Roger I . . . I've never been confessor to a woman.

Agnés Please. It seems this kingdom's at the mercy of the Vikings; wild, savage killers sweeping over hills, raping, burning . . . We're crawling along in an open cart, prey to every danger. It would comfort me to know I could confess, if I was going to die.

Roger I – Silence, would you sit with me?

Silence What's the matter?

Roger (*attempting to stand*) I'm a little dizzy. It'll pass.

Agnés He's going to faint!

Roger Good lady, it's – (*He faints.*)

TEN

A dungeon.

Ethelred (*filthy and alone*) Guard! Guard! Let me out,
you peasant, I'm your king! They found me dazed and
crownless, lying in a drain. They locked me here with the
rubbish of creation, thinking me a madman or a knave!
It is a portent . . . God's destruction is coming and order
is flung upside down. Pagans marry saints and kings rub
their faces in the mire. We are truly on the brink of the
end! How may I prevent it? What must I do? Ymma,
you came like salvation into my dream. You had to *hit*
me to make me see! I must not be afraid. I must take my
power. I must earn, with action, the taste of your music
in my mouth. I will break my chains and hurl them
away!! (*to the guard*) I am Ethelred Rex! Free me, you
slave, or I will *murder* you! . . .

ELEVEN

The cart.
   *Eadric and Ymma in the front. Roger has a cowl over
his head, protecting his eyes from the view. He resembles
the figure of Death.*

Eadric On the third day, she sat with me. We passed
through the outskirts of London at dawn. The walls still
had skulls of the Viking dead on view, from their failed
siege of '94. They will never take this marvellous city,
those cunts.

Ymma It stank like a witch's latrine. London . . . What a
dump.

Roger (*to Silence*) What is the Eucharist?

45

Agnés Our priest had decided to test the young lord on his catechism and a marvellous comfort came over me, listening to them speak.

Roger The Eucharist, Silence. We did it yesterday.

Agnés Although it was amazing how little the young lord knew.

Eadric She is silent. Her back straight in some kind of a royal way they must teach them from the cradle.

Silence The Eucharist is when God . . .

Ymma Where is the king? Every day I think today he will find us and he'll be revenged.

Eadric He'll never find us.

Ymma Why do you think that?

Eadric This cart is blessed and safe from harm.

Silence Turns himself into bread!

Roger (*sighs*) Silence . . . you must find the right words. It is the language of respect.

Eadric Every time I try to speak to her I –

Ymma What manner of man is the king?

Eadric He is a king. They cannot be judged like others. Sometimes, when I'm on duty at his door, I hear his thoughts. They come to me in purple.

Ymma Right.

Silence The Eucharist is the sacrament in which the Lord Jesus God is . . . baked?

Roger NO! Come on, Silence!

Silence In which . . .

Agnés . . . the soul and divinity of Our Lord is contained in the appearance of bread and wine! Sorry, Father, I couldn't help it. I love the catechism. I used to win prizes.

Eadric Every time I try to speak to her I –

Ymma (*pointing*) What's that?

Eadric It's the monastery of St Alban, where we may rest tonight. It's full of monks. They're famed for their devout lifestyle and their bee keeping. I find myself talking shit. It makes me hate myself.

Silence As I watched Eadric Longshaft, I suddenly realised who he reminded me of. He was the Barbarian, the Barbarian in the forest . . .

TWELVE

Canterbury.
    Ethelred is dressed in state, sitting on his throne, caressing it.

Ethelred I lay in my own dungeons for three days and three nights. I came within an inch of severing the thin cord of sanity which keeps our souls intact. When the bishops finally freed me, I put a knife to my gaoler's throat and ask him who was king. 'You!' he squealed – and in that word, I finally perceived the meaning of power. He who can inspire fear, is powerful. Like God. I cut his throat and felt myself grow stronger every second of his dying. The world is a different place to me now. I, Ethelred Rex, have realised the nature of God. And with this realisation comes the course of action I must take. God is as cruel as the jaws of the wolf. God is force. His word is chaos. And his will? His will be done.

THIRTEEN

The cart.
    Three days later. Rain. Ymma next to Eadric, Roger under his cowl, Agnés eating.

Roger Lesson twenty-two: Hell.

Agnés It had rained without break for three days. In places, the road was like a river bed.

Ymma We crawled across the belly of England.

Roger Hell is eternal, a place of perpetual dark.

Silence I'd had enough of learning the priest's faith. I wanted to sit in the front with Eadric.

Roger It is the hopeless destination of the damned.

Silence I had an urge to – (*She giggles.*) I wanted to see what he'd do. Perhaps he'd –

    Silence's imagination music. The sun comes out. She caresses the back of Eadric's neck. He turns and pulls her into the front of the cart. She lies in his arms, delighted, as Roger continues.

Roger In order to imagine Hell, one must think of the worst pain our soft flesh can suffer, the worst degradation our human spirits can bear and magnify it to eternity. One must think of an exhausting pitch of agony strung out like a screech until Doomsday.

Silence Eadric, I can't. My wife . . .

Eadric Don't ask me to control myself. I love you too much.

    Eadric kisses Silence. Silence swoons as Roger continues:

Roger Hell is a burning lake, vaster than all the seas, where God sends those who offend him; heathens, sinners, abominations of every kind!

Silence looks up. The sun goes in. She returns to the back of the cart and listens.

Roger God is terrible in his judgement! Once damned to Hell, there is no prayer and no penitence that will move him.

Silence Father, supposing that one was a heathen or an abomination – or both – and yet not a bad person. What would God do?

Roger He would damn you.

Silence But you said he loved all men.

Roger Yes, he may love them, but he won't save them. He's loving but cruel, omnipotent but heartlesss, benign but a force of terror! – I'm sorry!

Silence What is it?

Roger (*crumbling into distress*) We have to stop! I've upset myself . . .

Agnés (*to Roger, concerned*) May I offer you some cheese?

Roger No no no . . .

Agnés Or some dates? They come from the Holy Land. I like to think our Lord was comforted with dates, when he was in the desert.

Roger (*he takes a date*) You're very kind.

Eadric How proud she is in the rain, as if she drinks it with her skin.

Ymma The king could have caught us ten times over, don't you think?

Eadric I have told you what I think. You do not listen.

Ymma Perhaps he awoke from that punch and remembered nothing . . . I hardly dare to hope.

Eadric (*putting his jacket over Ymma's knees*) An offering of comfort, lady.

Ymma (*flinching*) What?

Eadric It's buckskin – waterproof.

Ymma No thank you. (*She pushes the jacket away.*)

Eadric But you're wet. Your garments, wet and clinging –

Ymma I said no.

Eadric Is it not good enough? Even for your knees?

Ymma Listen. I am grateful for your help. I appreciate everything you've done, but as far as I'm concerned, you are here to drive this cart. When we get to Cumbria, my husband will pay you for your service, and then you can trot back to your boyfriend, the king.

Eadric yanks the reins in a sudden fury. The cart goes out of control. It careers into a ditch. Roger is flung into the arms of Agnés. Eadric falls on top of Ymma.

Silence (*excited*) A cart crash! We'd gone off the road!

Roger (*to Agnés*) Dear lady – forgive me.

Agnés (*hurt*) It's nothing.

Roger Your food!

Ymma Get off me. Get off!

Eadric (*holding her down*) You speak me wrong. Listen!

Eadric doesn't move. He stares at Ymma with such intensity that she is afraid. She struggles.

Ymma DOG!

Eadric abruptly climbs off the cart. Ymma is extremely shaken.

Silence What's the matter? No wonder he's angry. You treat him like an animal. If you don't like him you should let me sit with him.

Ymma Stay away from him, Silence.

Silence Why should I?

Ymma Because I say so! (*She walks away.*)

Silence Don't order me around. You're my wife, not my mother!

Eadric I need help.

Silence (*jumping off the cart*) What can I do?

Eadric Wheel's fucked.

Agnés We were at the edge of a great moor. The wind was bitter and the rain poured.

Eadric (*to Roger*) Get out.

Roger I'll remain under here, good Sir. I suffer with weak lungs and I fear –

Eadric Out!

Roger (*climbing out, eyes shut*) There was nothing for it but to close my eyes and pretend that I was blind. I resolved not to open them again until we were safely installed in –

Ymma There's a cave here – we can shelter in it.

Roger Thank God!

Silence That's not a cave. It's a barrow.

Ymma What's a barrow?

Silence A tomb, where the ancient people buried their dead. Surr found one in Cumbria, full of skulls and weapons and the folded bones of a great eagle.

Agnés There'll be ghosts! Horrible shadowy things that suck men's souls!

Roger (*approaching*) Let me go in, dear ladies. I can hold up the cross of our Lord and bless the ground. Shadows will not harm you then. (*Barges past them into the cave. Loudly*) I am a priest. My name is Roger. Flee, things of night, in the name of God! (*Kneels.*) Let these rock walls close around me and keep me from that overwhelming sky. Oh please, please you pagan devils keep me safe inside. I'll drink blood in your service if you keep me here, just for a night, just for an hour. Blind me, have my soul, make me your creature but keep me from the nightmare of that moor . . .

FOURTEEN

The barrow.

Silence It took Eadric and I two hours to mend the wheel. The whole time he never spoke a word, except to say –

Eadric Give me that thing.

Silence He smelt of horses and rain and firewood and I kept thinking of my dream . . . See me Eadric, see me for what I am.

Agnés We curled up in the barrow that night, all five of us. It was a terrible squeeze. I found myself next to the priest. (*She settles.*)

Roger Our small candle cast shadows dancing across paintings of the ancient people – a leaping deer and a man with huge eyes, naked, holding a simple spear. He looked like our first father Adam, before the Fall. A feeling of peace came over me as I looked at him. (*Whispers.*) Pagan, pagan, I consign my soul to your care. (*He settles to sleep.*)

Agnés (*asleep*) Mm, yes . . .

Eadric (*watching Ymma.*) Words have always caught me in their snares. They betray me even as they spill from my mouth. Words are the instruments of lies. One day, all humanity will communicate with thought, for the mind speaks the truth, always. It's for this reason that I practise the art of mindspeech. (*He concentrates.*)

Agnés   . . . Yes, harder, there . . .

Eadric I find a dark space inside and imagine my message, like a beam of light travelling through the void. It leaves the sphere of my skull and like a lighted arrow, finds a route to the mind of the receiver . . . There are some who can speak over distances of miles, but I, who am a novice at the art, must be close. I am close now. My thoughts wind around her like a shroud. (*He whispers.*) Beloved, hear me . . .

Eadric closes his eyes. Pause. Ymma stirs. Pause. He touches her ankle. She wakes. She recoils.

Ymma (*pause*) Stay away from me, or I will kill you. I mean it.

Eadric Your words mean nothing. Only your thoughts.

Ymma If you touch me, I will kill you. Stay away!

Silence moans and puts her arm around Ymma. Ymma turns and kisses her.

Ymma Silence, I love you, my God-given gift . . .
Nothing must come between us.

Silence You strange creature. Strange, strange creature . . .

Their kisses become more passionate. Eadric, furious, leaves the cave. He goes to the cart, opens a bag of Ymma's clothes and starts to tear one of her dresses. He stops. He holds the dress to his face. He falls to his knees. He is going to make love to the dress.

FIFTEEN

A ship.

Ethelred I am full of the fire of revelation tonight. Perhaps it's the motion of this ship, or perhaps my clarity is God-given. As we cleave the waves, the whole journey of my life is rippling around me. I was sat on a blood-stained throne when I was ten years old; they padded the crown to make it fit. And the Vikings, seeing the land in the hands of a child, began their raids. They have blighted my life from the start. God's will is simple. I will drive that Viking blight from my shores. I will root out His pagan foes and do His apocalypse for Him. The boy Silence, as fresh-faced as I was when they made me king, is the crux of my revenge; he lies at the end of my path. The prize for his murder is Ymma. If the wind keeps with us, we'll be in Yarmouth at dawn. Then Hull, then Tynemouth. At this rate, I'll be in Cumbria before them.

SIXTEEN

Dawn. Outside the barrow.
   Birds tweeting. Roger is kneeling in Silence's un-Christian way.

Roger Help me, help me, help me, help me –

Agnés (*enters*) Father, I've just had a wonderful dream.

Roger I cannot interpret dreams or hear confessions – or do anything right now, I'm sorry!

Agnés I don't want you to interpret it; I just thought you might like to hear it. I was lying in a boat in the middle of the ocean and all I could see were tumbling waves and the great vault of the sky. I had a sense of being the tiniest thing in all creation.

Roger Oh –

Agnés There I was, no more than a dot in God's immense design –

Roger Ng!

Agnés – and suddenly, I could hear angelic singing . . .

Roger (*taken aback*) . . . Angelic singing?

Agnés When I was at the convent, our Abbess once said to me that angelic singing could only be heard by humankind in its dreams. She said that all of man's earthly music was merely an attempt to remember its fleeting beauty . . . It's strange how dreams can affect us. I've been so troubled on this journey but I think that hearing such music in a pagan tomb can only be an omen for something good.

Roger I pray it is. (*Lifts his cowl to see her.*) Forgive me – did you say you used to be a nun?

Agnès I was a foundling. The nuns cared for me. I lived with them until I was ten, then my lady's sainted mother purchased me and gave me to her daughter as a maid.

Roger My parents gave me to the bishops at the same age. Sold me into a worthy life.

Agnès It's the same for all the children of the poor. We have no freedom, do we?

Roger Lady, may I ask, if the question is not too intrusive: when you left your convent, did you by any chance, after such a long period of incarceration in a safe and familiar place, find yourself – oh this sounds so foolish! – did you find yourself unnerved, frightened, perhaps shaking in an unfathomable way at the sight of – fields?

Agnès (*understanding*) Oh . . .

Roger Did you find yourself yearning to be anywhere that would take your eyes from the swoon of the horizon, from the sheer, shuddering size of it? And when approaching an open moor, such as the one that looms ahead, did you ever find yourself praying that a mist might surround you, an eclipse, a cloud, anything, that you might not feel so horribly exposed to the endless land and the unspeakable vault of the sky?

Agnès Well, it's a long time ago but –

Roger And did you feel, when you were flung from the safety of all you held dear, that the nature of God had changed, that he was not the God you'd always believed in, not the friend you could rely on, but a wild stranger – or worse – did you begin to doubt his very existence, to feel the universe was so cruel and so chaotic that some other force must preside over it, some heartless, savage deity worshipped by the heathens who made this tomb – or worse – nothing at all, a heaven empty of divinity, a chaos of life with no guiding hand? Did you ever feel that the sky could be godless?

Agnés (*moved*) Yes, I did! Not because of the land, but because of where fate had thrown me. It made me despair.

Roger My dear sister, tell me, did these terrible feelings leave you?

Agnés Yes. But they change you. I fought hard to reconcile myself with God. There's nothing else to believe in, is there? (*Roger sobs.*) Father . . . you're crying. (*She puts out a hand.*)

Roger (*he clings to it*) Help me. Help me, help me . . .

SEVENTEEN

The cart.
   Eadric is asleep under Ymma's clothes. Silence enters.

Silence Eadric. Longshaft, wake up. What are you doing? These are my wife's clothes.

Eadric (*wakes with a jolt.*) I was cold . . .

Silence Oh, (*picking up a dress*) she was wearing this the first time I saw her, when she called me a boy and sneered. Look at that colour . . . (*Holds the dress against herself.*) Do you like it?

Eadric What?

Silence This shade – is it good? (*She giggles coyly.*)

Ymma (*entering*) What are you doing?

Silence (*showing Ymma the dress*) Look.

Ymma Silence –

Silence Eadric slept out here. He didn't have a blanket so he used your clothes.

Ymma (*to Eadric*) Is that true? (*Pause*) Did you touch my clothes? Answer me!

Eadric picks up a petticoat. He presses it to his cheek. Ymma is horrified.

Agnés, AGNÉS!

Agnés is elsewhere with Roger. He is holding on to her arm.

Agnés And this is mugwort; a humble plant but marvellous in the treatment of warts.

Ymma (*to Eadric*) Get away from my things!

Silence Ymma, what's he done?

Ymma Can't you see?

Agnés The detail of the moor will help you cross it. If you focus your eyes on all the tiny living things, the size of it won't trouble you.

Roger Look, a frog!

Ymma AGNÉS! (*to Eadric*) I feel sick when I look at you. Do you understand? DOG! How dare you violate my things!

Eadric gets off the cart. He exits. Agnés and Roger approach.

Agnés (*to Ymma*) What?

Ymma Get on the cart. Pick up my clothes. Take them over there.

Agnés What for?

Ymma Burn them.

Agnés *What?*

Ymma Burn them!

Silence Ymma, why?

Ymma Because they're *filthy*!

Agnés I'm not burning your clothes!

Roger These garments are objects of splendour. It would be a tragedy even to singe them!

Ymma Did I ask your opinion?

Roger No –

Ymma Then shut up! BURN THEM!

Silence No one's going to burn your clothes. I won't allow it!

Ymma Damn you, Silence, you stupid, naive fool!

Silence That's enough! You're my wife, Ymma, and you'll do what I say!

Ymma (*shocked*) Don't ever speak to me like that. You've NO RIGHT!

She exits. Pause. Silence bursts into snotty tears.

Roger Silence, my friend, do not cry . . .

Agnés (*drawing Roger away*) Sooner or later I knew this would happen.

Roger What?

Agnés One of her rages. They take her to the very brink of madness. In her last one, she tried to kill her brother – fell on him with a knife, tore him. It's why he sent her here. Father, I want to confess: I hate her for dragging me with her. I'm full of resentment, full of envious thoughts. If I were her, I'd find it so easy to be happy.

She's blessed with wealth and a beautiful face, yet she hates her life. I should pity her, but I can't. She holds my chains. (*to Silence, kindly*) Now, my lord. Dry your tears. What do you wish me to do?

EIGHTEEN

The moor.
   Ymma is vomiting. She finishes. She wipes her mouth. Eadric approaches.

Eadric It's hard being near you, lady.

Ymma Then keep away.

Eadric You make me forget myself.

Ymma How many women have you raped, Eadric? I know men like you. How many?

Eadric None.

Ymma Liar.

Eadric I say the truth.

Ymma Do you know what it means, rape?

Eadric Yes.

Ymma What?

Eadric I'll say it silently.

Ymma Rape means living through your own murder. No one will ever do it to me again. They're burning my clothes. Everything you touched will burn. Do you understand?

Eadric Listen.

   He falls to his knees and closes his eyes. Ymma impatiently leaves.

(*mindspeaking*) I was a boy. The Vikings came with a hundred ships. They burned the town and caused terror. We fought them in the mud by the sea. They slew us. I ran. Three of them found me. They held me down. Like a pig. That is rape, lady. You may trample me. You may walk on my back with your rage. Please.

Silence enters. Eadric opens his eyes. Ymma has gone. Silence is watching him.

Silence Are you praying?

Eadric No.

Silence Where's Ymma?

Eadric Gone.

Silence She asked me to burn her clothes. I couldn't. The priest said why not leave them as a sacrifice to the gods of the tomb, so that's what we've done. I don't understand her, Eadric. I don't understand women at all. I understand you better. You're a man.

Silence gently touches Eadric's shoulder. He looks at her. She half smiles. She leaves. Eadric tries to wipe Silence's touch from his body. He spits.

NINETEEN

Hull.

Ethelred Hull: a stinking village of rotting fish. The men of Kent swept out of their boats before me. I'd tasked them with rounding up Vikings but the people swore there were none; they hadn't had a Viking raid in years. We knew they were lying; they were all Vikings – you could tell by their shifty eyes. At last we found an old man with a rune on his hand; the mark of a Norse devil.

It's not a rune, he said, it's a ruptured vein. I quieted him
with my fist. He had five great sons and I ordered them
all stripped and tied. I found a different way of killing
every one. My men whooped and cheered; I'm still on
fire with the thought of it. As each one screamed his death,
I came nearer understanding the thrill of the divine.
I took their souls, like God. I grow more powerful by
the hour.

TWENTY

The cart.
   *Silence and Eadric in the front. Ymma sits alone,
facing backwards.*

Roger As we left the moor, I saw a small, brown bird
pulling worms from the ground. It looked at me with
eyes full of eloquence and seemed to say, 'Lo Roger, the
wilderness is alive with purple flowers and the dew-
strung webs of spiders.' The next day we crossed a
stream of clear waters which I wanted to leap from the
cart and touch. Rabbits. The evening thronged with
rabbits. They reminded me of myself.

Silence My wife was silent. She seemed to be in a
different place and not with us in the cart at all. It was
like being with a stranger.

Eadric Dog.

Roger And then we entered a forest.

Silence The light came horizontal through the trees.

Roger For days, we gazed at a rich canopy of flaming
colours. An ochre leaf dropped from a branch and
landed in my lap. It was soft and lined, like the palm
of my hand.

Agnés It's lucky.

Roger Lucky?

Agnés Very lucky. To catch an autumn leaf.

Roger Ah. (*He gives it to Agnés.*) May the luck belong to you.

Agnés is moved.

Silence (*joining Ymma*) Ymma, I hate this. Why are you using your silence against me?

Ymma Because I fear . . . that if I try to speak . . . it won't be a word that comes out of my mouth but a madwoman's shriek. I know these times of old. It's as if the world turns to ash and a chasm yawns between living things and me.

Silence Ymma, you can't talk like this! What do you mean?

Ymma I mean I'm nothing. I'm a thing that sits to be looked at, a thing that mustn't think. I mean my brother held me down, hand over mouth, and showed me the purpose for which I was born. (*She can't speak.*)

Silence Ymma. (*She takes Ymma in her arms.*)

Ymma I'm a pool, a dark glass into which men can peer and see themselves as strong. Let dark waters wash over me. Let me be ash. Let me be dust and disappear.

TWENTY-ONE

Tynemouth.

Ethelred Round up all those Viking-born and slay them! I don't care how many generations they've lived here; if they've been tilling the land since Alfred's time it's not long enough. They are not your brothers! They will never be sons of England and their loyalty will never be to this nation or this crown. They have taken our land and raped it, and until they are gone, we will never be free. Beloved people, I commend you to God, for his judgement is cruel. Pray he might not send it before we purge these savages from our shores. Men of England, march with me on the road to righteous murder! March with me to Cumbria! (*Pause.*) That was Tynemouth. I was brilliant. Filthy people kissed my hand and cheered. No one could believe it was me.

TWENTY-TWO

York.

Roger At the other end of the forest was the city of York –

Ymma (*jumping off the cart*) A dump.

Agnés A marvellous town, full of Roman buildings; quite the busiest place I ever saw. It seemed that one could buy anything here.

Silence Ymma, where are you going?

Ymma Wait for me. (*Exits.*)

Silence I began to feel our journey was in its final stage. At last, we were in the North!

Eadric Look at it. Viking shit. I wish all Vikings dead, dead and buried in a great stinking pit of my making.

Silence I'm a Viking.

Eadric I know. (*He spits.*)

Silence (*hurt*) He told me to –

64

Eadric Sit in the cart and guard it!

Silence So I did.

Eadric exits.

Agnés The priest and I took the opportunity to walk along the city walls. We looked at the view below us, a forested vale, as far as the eye could see.

Roger Naked winter trees. Such dignity in their bareness. You've reconciled me with the horizon. I don't know how to thank you.

Agnés Oh, it was nothing . . .

Roger Dear lady,

Agnés For both of us, it was a moment of –

A note of angelic music. They exit. Silence alone.

Silence What am I? I cannot be a husband to my wife. I cannot be a woman to a man. I am nothing. No wonder he spits at me. If only I could tell him that underneath I – Eadric . . . I'm sick of hiding. I want to be free. Help me.

Ymma enters, dressed as a man.

Ymma Silence? Do you like it? I was inspired by you.

Silence What did you do with your dress?

Ymma I traded it.

Silence Your last dress?

Ymma Yes. It's gone, every nun-made stitch of it.

Silence Ymma, I wish you'd traded anything else! Your last dress . . .

Ymma What about it?

Silence I wanted it.

Ymma What for?

Silence To see myself! . . . To see what I look like.

Ymma Oh, Silence . . .

Silence How can I know myself until I've seen myself? I don't know who or what I am!

Ymma You are Silence of Cumbria! Silence . . . We'll soon be home, my love. You have the whole future to know yourself.

Eadric enters, laden with supplies. He sees two men embracing.

Eadric Sodomites. (*He draws his sword, disgusted.*)

Ymma Are you going to murder us, cabbage?

Agnés (*entering with Roger*) Ymma, what are you doing dressed like that?

Ymma Look. (*She kicks the air in front of Eadric's face.*) Freedom. You might think about doing the same. We're going into wild lands and I want to protect myself.

Roger Ah. (*to Agnés*) Should I dress as a man, do you think?

Ymma Sit with me in the front, Silence. Teach me to drive the cart.

TWENTY-THREE

Ragnarok.

Ethelred Our march through Cumbria was triumphant. We slaughtered the heathen and pride was in our step. We came to the runt's castle with our banners unfurled and I, dressed in my finest furs, was carried aloft – my travel throne placed on a bier. The place was abandoned.

66

The heathens must have heard of our approach and fled.
I entered alone – as befits a warrior king – and in the
hall, by a great fire, sat a solitary woman. She said she
was a priest – but by the robes she wore and the
mistletoe twined in her hair, I could see she was a witch.
I felt power surging through me, fabulous power, power
of life and death. My hands were itching for a murder.
I expected her to shriek, or spit, or beat herself with a
sacred fish – but she did nothing. She stood silently,
eyeing me. It was . . . audacious. It was then I had another
revelation about power. Sometimes, to kill is not enough.
One has to torture first.

TWENTY-FOUR

A barn.
  Eadric is serving stew around a fire.

Silence We were less than a day from my home, high in
the mountains of Cumbria: my home.

Roger We stopped by the shores of a darkening lake,
and as the heavens stretched out in a glorious canopy of
winter stars, we made our camp in a disued barn.

Eadric Stew.

Roger Delicious. It's inspiring to watch a man cook.
Makes me think men can do anything!

  Ymma spits a bone out. She wipes her nose on her
  sleeve.

Silence Somehow, with her dressed like that, there
seemed to be no difference between us.

Ymma One day, maybe not for a hundred years, maybe
not for two, all women will be driving loaded carts up
hills. That's my dream, Silence.

Silence I thought her more beautiful than ever. And if she was beautiful dressed as a man, then maybe I was, too.

Eadric I can hear her. In the high air, her thoughts have come, curling round me like a mist. 'Lord Silence is a sodomite,' she says. 'For him, I have rubbed my female nature in the mud. Help me, Eadric. Return me to my natural state.'

Ymma burps loudly. Eadric looks at her, with understanding.

Eadric Tonight I will lift her high once more. Tonight, we will have truth and truth and truth. I've put three hundred mystic mushrooms in the stew.

Roger The season of Yule is upon us and the more I look at our humble surroundings, the more I'm reminded of our Lord's nativity.

Agnés Oh yes, born in a barn.

Roger When our meal is over I should like to say Mass – to celebrate the end of our journey and to thank God for keeping us safe.

Ymma Our journey isn't over yet. You've seen the villages we've passed: blackened shells, corpses rotting in the fields. There's Vikings everywhere. Why thank God about that? You should keep your prayers 'til you're safe in Ragnarok.

Eadric It's not Vikings.

Ymma What?

Eadric Those villages. Vikings kill different.

Silence He's right. Vikings cut runes into dying flesh as offerings to the gods.

Eadric The corpses I looked at are normal. Like we make. In Kent.

Ymma The king . . .

Silence There's always people raiding round here. It could be the Strathclyde Welsh, or the Celts or the crazy people from the Isle of Man. We'll be safe in Ragnarok. The walls are as high as trees.

Agnés Why don't you say the Mass? It would be such a comfort to us all, Roger . . .

Roger Dear lady, of course.

Eadric The mushrooms began to take effect during the sermon.

Roger Brothers and sisters, dear brothers and dear sisters, my friends, here we are, five humble souls, protected only by a barn in a land where violence rages and chaos seems to rule.

Eadric begins to undress himself.

There are those who say this chaos is a sign. They say God is sending his destruction, preparing his vials of wrath to pour upon the Earth. The skies will darken, fires will roar and there'll be nowhere, nowhere to hide . . . So that, my dear friends, is my question for this evening. Is God going to destroy us? And if he is, is he wrong?

When Eadric is naked from the waist up, he begins to oil his torso.

Because . . . because I think he is. How could he even think of destroying us? It's an outrage. If he wanted us perfect, why did he create us flawed? And if he created us flawed, why does he blame us for it? God is *wrong*! We live lives of such misery, punishing ourselves in his name. Is his thanks to send destruction? Frankly, if it was the other way round, if we had the power to obliterate him, I wouldn't hesitate. Rid the world of God, I say, rid it of fate and shame; let all deities be gone! My friends, we may be only days away from the end. How should we behave? Should we gouge our cheeks and rub ashes into our hair? Should we wail out our sins like starving wolves in the snow? I say no! I say if destruction is coming then taste the life you never had. Pluck it like a late apple and lets its tartness fill your mouth. Gorge yourselves on the scent of blown roses, lick frost from spider's webs, smash the ice on drinking troughs and hurl it in splinters at the sun. I say glory in the world, exult in nature, immerse yourself in womankind!

Agnés Amen!

Roger Dear lady . . .

Agnés I love you!

They embrace.

Come outside. I want to show you something.

Agnés and Roger exit. The sound of drums begins, gradually coming nearer.

Silence After Mass, my wife developed a golden halo. And –

Eadric draws his broadsword. He swishes it around.

Eadric did that. The ground's becoming the sea . . . I'm fine really. (*She collapses.*)

Eadric I was reckless that night. The barn was filled with the shadow of goats. (*He points his sword at Ymma.*) I will see you dishonoured no longer.

Ymma You put drugs in that stew, didn't you?

70

Eadric The mushrooms of truth. I know what you want of me.

Ymma What are you talking about? I want nothing!

Eadric Your freedom. (*He advances.*) Say with your mouth what I know from your mind and I'll plaster the roof with his guts, now, while he sleeps: let me, now!

Ymma No! NO!

Silence (*standing, with her sword drawn.*) Ha! Unhand my wife . . . big man.

Ymma Silence, he's drugged you.

Silence I will fight you, Frost Giant.

Ymma He means you harm!

Silence I am a thing of the forest, fleet of foot and sharp of eye.

Ymma Put down the sword and get out!

Silence See me for what I am. See my nature, Eadric!

Ymma Silence!

Silence Away with you, wife! This is man's affair.

Ymma (*she shouts*) AGNÉS! . . . Bring the priest! PRIEST! . . .

Silence I'll meet you in Valhalla, barbarian.

Ymma (*attempts to stop her*) What are you *doing*?

Eadric Let him fight! And when I've killed him, I'll get those fucking goats over there!

> *Silence lunges at Eadric. He soon disarms her. He picks her up, in a tight hold.*

Silence Eadric . . .

Ymma (*screeching*) Silence, what are you *doing*?

Silence kisses Eadric. He drops her, disgusted, and with instinctive violence, he pulls out his dagger. Ymma throws herself between them.

No, NO! He's drugged; it's not his fault! He thought he was kissing me! Me, Eadric!

Eadric (*about to plunge in the dagger*) It said my name!

Ymma stops Eadric's mouth with a kiss. Eadric is paralysed by the force of it. Silence backs away as the kiss continues. And continues. At last Ymma breaks off. Eadric gazes at her.

Ymma Silence, get out. Run.

Silence exits, distressed.

You love me, don't you?

Eadric nods. Without breaking the gaze, Ymma takes his dagger. She stands.

I've never thanked you properly for the way you saved me in Canterbury, for the way you led us here, so bravely. You hide a lot in your silence, don't you? (*Eadric embraces Ymma's legs.*) There . . . (*She strokes him.*) What a shining soul you must have. You're strong, you're noble and you never lie, do you? Maybe my feelings could grow . . . (*She raises the dagger.*)

Roger (*entering*) There's drums!

Agnés (*following*) Coming up the valley!

Eadric flings himself in front of Ymma and picks up his sword.

Roger A band of men with flaming torches!

Eadric (*turning on Roger*) Draw, Priest!

Roger Merciful God!

Eadric Keep your goats at bay!

Agnés Listen! Drums!

The drums are close, and getting louder.

Eadric Move, now!

Agnés They're Vikings!

Eadric Worse. They're men of Kent.

Ymma (*at the door*) Silence! SILENCE!

Eadric Where's my fucking shirt?

Agnés Run! Hide!

Ymma SILENCE! . . .

Roger and Eadric pull her away.

TWENTY-FIVE

In the snow.

Silence (*alone, running*) Abomination! Stupid and naive!
I am so WRONG! He would have *killed* me . . . She is
the only one, the only one who doesn't judge me, the
only one who wants me to be free. My bride, my bride
who saves me with her kiss! YMMA! . . . I don't know
how long I ran. Towards morning, it began to snow.
I ran and ran, through the darkness, long into the
spinning light of day. I was flying! My mind soared,
snowlight swirled around me and dazzling iceflakes
melted on my tongue. (*slowing down*) At last I came to a
forest, white and silent in a shroud of snow. The air was
hushed and branches closed round me like a veil. And
then I realised . . . These were trees I knew, summer and

winter, familiar as the veins on my hands! This was my forest! – And there, looming out of the shade, its dark shape outlined in frost, was Ragnarok, my home! YMMA! Wife of my HEART! We're HERE!

Act Three
Cumbria

TWENTY-SIX

Ragnarok.

Ethelred After thirty hours, the witch was nearly dead.
I had slept and watched, dreamt and listened in a daze
of fascination, as my men expertly broke her. To keep
myself amused, I began to tell her what she might expect
on the Day of Judgement. But she said: 'This, now, is
judgement. This is the winter and every winter is the
winter without end.' I questioned her as to what she
meant. It appears that in her theology, the end begins
when our mother, the sun, is torn out of the sky by a
ravenous wolf. The world freezes and we perish in
endless dark and cold. Every winter they fear it: an
apocalypse of ice. They only know they have escaped
it with the first warmth of spring. This wolf, this giant
evil, is the very spirit of chaos. I've been meditating on
his image; it is indeed powerful. So, as the wolf howls
with victory in the darkness, Odin and the hordes of
Valhalla meet him for the final battle on the frozen seas.
No one wins. All is destroyed, matter, spirit, evil, good,
everything, utterly lost. As the witch died, she told me
that the last act of Odin, with the jaws of the wolf
around his neck, is to fling fire over the world. 'It'll end
in flames,' she said. 'Everything will end in flames.' 'And
afterwards?' I asked, but she was dead. An eternity of
nothing, I suppose. The concept of salvation is too
refined for these barbarians.

*A light comes up on Silence. She is kneeling, her
hands tied behind her.*

What do you make of it, Lord Silence? There's not a lot of dignity in torture – but your witch impressed us all. I've hung her naked body from your walls, as a sign of our respect. Shall I do the same with you?

Silence It doesn't matter what you do. Surr isn't there on the walls and neither will I be if you kill me.

Ethelred You'll be burning in the fires of Hell.

Silence I don't believe in Hell.

Ethelred I must abandon you to an eternity of nothing, then.

Silence Odin's fire will melt the ice. And out of the water a new world will rise. The final flames become a new sun, who begins her journey across the sky. The end is the beginning. It continues world after world, life after life. The final destruction doesn't exist because life will defeat it in the end. That's what Surr was saying as she died. You are the wolf incarnate – but life will defeat you.

Ethelred The wolf incarnate. I like that.

Silence Life will tread upon your neck and the future will forget your name. I don't care what you do with me. This is my home. I know who I am here and I'm stronger than you. My curse on you, king. May the future laugh in your face.

Ethelred Let me show you the future, Lord Silence. Here it is, in my hand.

> *Ethelred brings down his fist on Silence's face. She collapses. Pause. He notices Eadric, who is kneeling before him. Ymma, Agnés and Roger have entered behind him. They stand in the shadows, staring at Silence.*

Eadric, what perfection! (*Hugs him.*) I knew you were close when I found this boy, skulking like a burglar at the gates. Here I am, like an eagle in my nest awaiting prey, and he delivers me himself!

Eadric We found villages; your work.

Ethelred Yes! I'm doing my own killing for the first time.

Eadric Our journey; you at the beginning and at the end.

Ethelred There's a symmetry in that. A kind of omnipotence, an alpha and omega.

Roger Sire, forgive me; I –

Ethelred Who's this?

Roger I am a – My name is Roger, Sire.

Ethelred Priest! You listened to my dream.

Roger Yes –

Ethelred It changed my life, that dream, put me on the path of truth.

Roger I am glad of it, but, Sire –

Ethelred God was speaking and you helped me hear him! I won't forget that, Priest.

Roger Let me ask you on my knees – Lord Silence – is he dead?

Ethelred Not yet.

Roger Sire – he's just a boy! / I plead for mercy – clemency and grace!

Ethelred Grace does not apply to heathens. He's a pagan, he's a traitor, he's venomous, he cursed me; I'd say he was kin to the Antichrist himself!

Ymma (*aside, to Agnés*) / What'll we do?

Agnés I don't know.

Ymma We have to get him out.

Agnés I can't do anything, can I?

Ymma Help me, Agnés, please, I beg you!

Agnés There's fifty men of Kent out there. How far d'you think you'll get?

Roger Please, your Majesty, if you murder this boy you will jeopardise your soul!

Ethelred Priest, it's not murder. When murder is justified it becomes something else.

Ymma (*drawing a sword*) Get away from him.

Ethelred (*noticing her*) YMMA!

Ymma Get back.

Ethelred What's *happened* to you?

Ymma Lord Silence is innocent of any wrong against you.

Ethelred You look AWFUL!

Ymma Let him go!

Ethelred Eadric, why is she dressed like this?

Eadric Not my fault.

Ethelred Priest, did you say nothing to her? You're supposed to be her spiritual guide!

Roger Well, it wasn't / my business. I –

Ethelred This is appalling! You look like a MAN! Something has to be done . . . (*to Agnés*) You, woman, where are her things?

Agnés Our cart was destroyed, Sire, by your men. There's nothing left.

Ethelred Well, that's no good!

Ymma Let him go!

Ethelred (*to Ymma*) I can't look at you dressed like that. I've come all the way up here pursuing your image and look what you've done!

Ymma I said release my husband!

Ethelred Get undressed!

Ymma What?

Ethelred (*to Agnés*) You, help her! Get that nightmare off! Eadric, take that thing from her, it's ridiculous! (*to Agnés*) You! MOVE! I'll avert my eyes until you resemble yourself.

Ymma Eadric, help me!

Eadric I am.

> *Eadric takes the sword. Agnés begins to undress Ymma.*

Agnés I'm sorry, my lady.

Ethelred (*to Eadric*) Eadric, take that boy away and kill him. I don't care how; just do it. Hang him, stab him, throw him from the tower, whatever. When the deed is done, come and tell me. I want you for my guard of honour, my best of men.

Roger Sire, the boy has never spoken treason or disloyalty –

Ethelred The boy is the past! You must look to the future, Priest. Your future may be very bright. I like you. You're insightful, compassionate; more truly a man of God than every bishop in this place.

Roger Sire, I have changed –

Ethelred I want you to marry me.

Roger Pardon?

Ethelred A union between us is God's will. I feel it in my heart and I know it with my soul. Our marriage will be sacred. I'm giving you the honour of conducting the service.

Roger Ah.

Ethelred Prepare for it, here, now! From now on, you are a bishop. (*to Eadric*) I gave you an order, Eadric! Move!

Eadric picks up Silence. Ymma is in her shift.

Ymma (*desperate*) Silence is a girl!

Eadric stops.

Silence of Cumbria is a girl, a young girl of fourteen.

Ethelred *What*?

Ymma She is sinless. Until our wedding night she was ignorant of her sex, ignorant of everything. Please, you must let her go.

Agnés is aghast. She looks at Silence anew.

Roger I am more shocked than I can say. This is a grievous, fatal lie. And it is cruel!

Ymma Oh, Priest, think! It's the truth!

Ethelred Why are you trying to save him? I'm doing you a favour!

Roger That is Silence, Lord of Cumbria, my student, my friend, my brother. Do not rob him of his dignity at the moment of his dying!

Ethelred Eadric, take him away.

Ethelred stops Ymma from intervening as Eadric takes Silence away.

(*his arms tightly around her*) My love, in a few minutes we'll be wed. Priest, prepare an altar. Let us be joined, one flesh, one blood. Let me melt in your deep depths . . .

Agnés She cannot marry you, I'm sorry.

Ethelred Did you address me?

Agnés I beg your pardon Sire, but she hasn't got a dress. You can't expect the daughter of a saint to marry a king in her shift. It's not dignified.

Ethelred She hasn't got a dress? . . .

Agnés No. Forgive me, but you must delay the wedding until she finds one.

Ethelred A dress. You are right . . . she must have a dress.

Agnés And a veil. And footwear. And all the garments for underneath. It's only proper.

Ethelred Yes, even though we are all naked before God, my wife shall have a dress. It will be my first gift to her. Silk, fur, jewels; she shall have everything . . . . Priest, we shall marry at midnight and consummate our union in the new dawn. Be ready. I go on a quest for your garments.

Ethelred kisses Ymma's hand. He leaves. Agnés peers after Silence and Eadric.

Agnés (*to Roger*) You fool!

Roger What?

Agnés Follow them. For God's sake, save her!

Comprehension dawns on Roger's face. He exits hurriedly after Silence and Eadric.

81

TWENTY-SEVEN

The tower.
    Eadric is walking up flights of stone stairs with Silence in his arms. A high wind blows.

Silence When I awoke, I was in his arms. The afternoon had fled and everything was dark. Even the snow was invisible . . . Eadric?

Eadric I will not hurt you.

Silence Are you going to let me go?

Eadric No. But I will cause you no pain.

Silence You'll kill me without pain?

Eadric The rocks you fall on will cause the pain, not me.

Silence You're going to throw me from the tower?

Eadric Without touching you.

Silence How will you do that?

Eadric With my mind. (*He releases Silence.*) Stand up.

Silence You will never make me jump.

Eadric Go to the edge.

Silence I'll leap of my own accord and fly forever.

Eadric Tell me what is down there.

Silence Darkness.

Eadric Then prepare to meet it.

    Roger appears. He is clutching Ymma's sword, afraid.

Silence I am full of colour. I love –

Roger Stand back, Eadric, or I will be forced to act!

Silence wavers. Roger tries to assist her.

Silence, child –

Silence NO!

Silence jumps.

Roger Silence! SILENCE, NO! God forgive me! God forgive me! Silence!

Roger exits.

Eadric Suicide.

He spits.

TWENTY-EIGHT

A bedchamber.
Agnés is dressing Ymma in an elaborate wedding gown.

Agnés As the hour of midnight approached, I was told to take her to a chamber and dress her in the clothes and jewels that the king had provided. It was unbearable. Ymma, there was nothing anyone could do.

Ymma (*pause*) Tighter. Make it hurt.

Agnés The only comfort I can offer is to say that for those who have faith, death is not –

Ymma Shut up. Don't you dare.

Agnés continues to dress Ymma. She is about to put on a necklace. She looks at it. Steals it.

Agnés (*pause*) Ymma, I'm going to leave you. I know this isn't a good time, but really, we've never been any good for one another and I have to go.

Ymma Pardon?

Agnés I'm sorry.

Ymma You're leaving me?

Agnés The priest and I are going to run away. We want to start a new life together.

Ymma The priest wants you for his wife?

Agnés Well he hasn't actually asked the question yet, but –

Ymma He won't marry you.

Agnés Why not?

Ymma How stupid are you, Agnés? He's going to be a bishop.

Agnés Yes, but –

Ymma The king is making him royal confessor – the most powerful cleric in the land. Do you think he'd throw all that away to go off into the dawn with you? Because what are you? What exactly are you, Agnés? A penniless maid with bedchamber skills.

Agnés Since I was ten years old, I've been living off crumbs from your life! No wonder I'm nothing! You've never cared –

Ymma Neither have you!

Agnés turns to go.

Agnés!

She grabs Agnés's hand. Neither speaks. Agnés pulls her hand away. She goes to the door.

Agnés You have it in you to rule this land. You know that, don't you? (*Pause.*) I'm sorry.

Agnés leaves. Ymma sits for a moment. She picks up a knife. She examines it. She walks into the centre of the space. She feels for her heart. She raises the knife. Eadric enters.

Eadric (*gently*) There is no need to do that, lady. I am here.

Ymma (*falters*) Eadric . . .

Pause. Eadric approaches her. He kneels.

Eadric I will do it. As you ask.

Ymma As I ask?

Eadric I hear you.

Ymma How? I've said nothing.

Eadric With your mind. The thought comes in like God-light. Help me.

Ymma I speak to you then, with my mind?

Eadric Yes.

Ymma I see . . . What am I saying now?

Eadric You're thanking me for killing Silence without pain. He fell from the tower, without pain.

Ymma (*pause. Swallows her grief*) Yes. I thank you.

Eadric You're thanking me also for this.

Ymma For what?

Eadric For what I am about to do. Treason. He will come in. And I will kill him.

Ymma I see. I thank you. And afterwards, when the treason is done; what then?

Eadric Then . . . you will open yourself, like an iris. And I will make sure you are sacred.

Ymma (*pause.*) Come to me, Eadric.

Eadric embraces Ymma's legs.

There . . .

She strokes him. She still has the knife. She raises it.

Eadric You're saying something else.

Ymma What? What else am I saying, my love?

Eadric Dog. You're calling me a dog.

Ymma Good dog . . .

Eadric (*standing, pulling her violently*) I AM NOT YOUR DOG!

Ymma stabs him with a scream. Eadric, wounded, won't let her go.

Eadric I am not . . . your dog!

Ymma Agnés, AGNÉS!

Eadric pulls Ymma on to the floor. He holds her as violently as he can, staring intently at her.

Eadric What am I?

Ymma screams.

BELOVED! Say it!

Ymma Brother . . . BROTHER!

Eadric Make her appear again.

Ymma What?

Eadric The shining lady. Make her appear . . .

Ymma There.

Ymma stabs him again. He slowly dies. Ymma is beneath him. She tries to move him. She can't.

Ymma Oh God . . . God help me!

Roger enters, dressed as a bishop in bright red robes.

Roger (*formally*) His Majesty the King.

Ethelred enters, sumptuously attired.

Ethelred Lady, the hour of midnight is almost upon us. I'm so emotional I can barely –

Roger Ymma! Sire! –

Ethelred Eadric, you BASTARD! What are you doing?

Roger and Ethelred run to Ymma's help. They lift Eadric away.

He's dead . . . My God, she's killed him. Ymma, why?

Ymma Take him away. Please.

Ethelred You, Bishop, get him out of here. Angel . . . what happened?

Roger Um. Forgive me, Sire. I'm not sure I can move him on my own.

Ethelred NOW!

Roger Of course, of course.

Roger drags Eadric away.

Ethelred Speak . . . what did he do?

Ymma He was going to hide in here and murder you.

Ethelred The son of a Kentish whore! He was my right hand! . . . Ymma, you saved me. You saved my life. Priest! She loves me and this proves it!

Roger (*off*) Marvellous, Sire.

Ethelred Oh my avenging angel, we shall be married at once.

Ymma I can't.

Ethelred Why not?

Ymma I'm a murderess. How can a murderess be a queen?

Ethelred My mother was a murderess and she was queen. Where is the problem?

Roger My lady is saying that she needs to confess. In order to be married, she must stand pure before God and as royal confessor, I must insist on hearing her sins.

Ethelred Yes . . . you are right. Bishop, she is yours. Inform me when she's redeemed and I'll return to make her my wife. (*He leaves.*)

Ymma Bless me, Father, for I have sinned.

Roger Lady –

Ymma I promised I would kill myself and I lied. I thought I wanted death, but I fought murder. I could have let him kill me, but I killed him! It means this: I would rather be alive than dead. I have chosen life without love, without freedom, with nothing to sustain me. Here is my sin: I have betrayed Silence and become life's whore.

Roger Lady, forgive me. I cannot take your confession. (*He takes off his mitre.*)

Ymma Why not?

Roger I'm no longer a priest. I have renounced the priesthood and all my vows. I am a man, this simple man you see before you. These clothes are but a costume from the king's canonical wardrobe. There is nothing sanctifying in them or in me. I feel like Adam, new created.

Ymma So, you are leaving me too?

Roger I am walking into Eden with my Eve . . . Agnés awaits me in the forest. I am hers. Oh lady, we have made miraculous plans.

Ymma Well, I'm glad. I'm truly glad . . .

Roger But we are worried at the thought of leaving you without a companion. Agnés has asked me to find someone to take her place. Not an easy task in these wild parts, but I met a young person by the walls this night, a person I think will suffice. She's a little rough, but in time you might teach her the ways of, well, womanish things.

Ymma Can she loosen a dress?

Roger I imagine that task would not be beyond her.

Ymma Then get her in.

Roger I shall leave you to prepare.

Ymma Priest –

Roger My name is Roger.

Ymma Thank you.

Roger shows Silence into the chamber. She is dressed in Agnés's clothes. He exits.

Ymma (*without looking round*) Undo this, would you? It's so tight, it's making me sick. Nuns made it. Bitches.

Silence begins to undo the dress.

Ymma (*sighs*) What's your name, girl? Speak up.

Silence I don't have one.

Ymma Then what shall I call you?

Silence makes no reply.

Silence.

89

She turns, she realises. They embrace.

Silence . . . Oh Silence, look at you. Please let me never wake.

Silence Ymma, it's amazing how quickly thoughts fly through your mind at the moment of your death. When I fell, my arms went out wide and for all the time it takes a mouse's heart to beat I gloried in my flying. I braced myself to hit the ground and finish – but my death was painless . . . There was simply nothing, nothing but cold. When I opened my eyes, I was lying in an underworld of ice. And then I heard the voice of the priest! He was trying to find me, begging God's forgiveness, really in a terrible state, wailing, crying . . . I was in snow! Feet and feet of snow! He picked me up, thanked his God for the miracle, and took me in to Agnés.

Ymma You strange creature. Strange, strange creature . . .

Silence We made a vow to be flesh and bone together. We should love and protect each other, don't you think?

Roger (*enters.*) His Majesty the King.

Ymma and Silence part. Ethelred enters. Silence begins to pin on Ymma's veil.

Ethelred My bishop says you are prepared. My love –

Ymma Your Majesty, dearly betrothed, kind king . . . I have some small requests to make before we are wed. May I beg your indulgence?

Ethelred You may beg anything.

Ymma When I am queen, I would like my own rooms.

Ethelred Your own rooms?

Ymma Where I receive you as a guest at my discretion. This way, you'll never tire of me. I wish to sit in all meetings of state, with my . . . companion, just to observe the world of men. I want to learn how a nation should be run.

Ethelred Bishop, why does she make these requests?

Roger She is a powerful woman, Sire, and they do come with certain drawbacks. But these seem like small enough requests. She saved your life, after all –

Ethelred Yes, Saviour, you shall have all you ask for. Now take my hand and with it my life, my crown, my England.

Ethelred and Ymma stand before Roger. Silence makes Ymma's veil fall around her. As Ymma marries Ethelred, she puts out a hand to Silence. Silence clasps it, tight.

Roger And the Lord caused a deep sleep to fall on Adam and he took one of his ribs and closed up the flesh thereof. And the rib, which the Lord God had taken from man, made he into a woman . . .

As the service continues, Agnés enters.

Agnés After the wedding, we fled. We never saw either of them again. Ymma remained consecrated queen for sixteen years and I believe that hardly ever, during all that time, was she parted from her companion, who was always silent in the company of the king but was often heard talking and laughing when alone with the queen. They seemed to speak a language no one else knew or understood. In the end, the king lost his throne to the Vikings and, when he died, Ymma married his Danish successor, Canute. She became one of the most powerful women of her age. The world didn't end.

Roger (*joins Agnés*) My theological ex-brothers are still convinced that Doomsday is looming. At any time an angel will open the bottomless pit and out of it will come pestilence, locusts and scorpions – and a great Beast who will wage war upon mankind! And the seas will boil and the streets will be littered with unburied dead and – forgive me; I have upset myself!

Agnés My husband is still troubled by apocalyptic dreams. I try to comfort him as best I can, but in my heart, I understand him.

She and Roger are gazing at one another.

They are the inevitable fears of our times, living as we do . . .

They move closer.

On the edge of destruction.

They kiss. Angelic music.

The End.

*Discover the brightest and best in fresh theatre writing
with Faber's new StageScripts*

Sweetheart by Nick Grosso   (0571 17967 3)
Mules by Winsome Pinnock   (0571 19022 7)
The Wolves by Michael Punter   (0571 19302 1)
Gabriel by Moira Buffini   (0571 19327 7)
Skeleton by Tanika Gupta   (0571 19339 0)
The Cub by Stephanie McKnight   (0571 19381 1)
Fair Game by Rebecca Prichard   (0571 19476 1)
(a free adaptation of **Games in the Backyard** by Edna Mazya)
Crazyhorse by Parv Bancil   (0571 19477 x)
Sabina! by Chris Dolan   (0571 19590 3)
I Am Yours by Judith Thompson   (0571 19612 8)
Been So Long by Che Walker   (0571 19650 0)
Yard Gal by Rebecca Prichard   (0571 19591 1)
Sea Urchins by Sharman Macdonald   (0571 19695 0)
Twins by Maureen Lawrence   (0571 20065 6)
Skinned by Abi Morgan   (0571 20007 9)
Real Classy Affair by Nick Grosso   (0571 19592 x)
Down Red Lane by Kate Dean   (0571 20070 2)
Shang-a-Lang by Catherine Johnson   (0571 20077 x)
The Storm by Alexander Ostrovsky
trs. Frank McGuinness   (0571 20004 4)
By Many Wounds by Zinnie Harris   (0571 20097 4)
So Special by Kevin Hood   (0571 20044 3)
The Glory of Living by Rebecca Gilman   (0571 20140 7)
Certain Young Men by Peter Gill   (0571 20191 1)
Paddy Irishman, Paddy Englishman and Paddy . . . ?
by Declan Croghan   (0571 20128 8)
Pelleas and Melisande by Maurice Maeterlinck
trs. Timberlake Wertenbaker   (0571 20201 2)
Martha, Josie and the Chinese Elvis
by Charlotte Jones   (0571 20237 3)
My Best Friend by Tamsin Oglesby   (0571 20566 6)
Dogs Barking by Richard Zajdlic   (0571 20006 0)
All That Trouble That We Had by Paul Lucas   (0571 20267 5)
The Bedsit by Paul Sellar   (0571 20364 7)
Drink, Dance, Laugh and Lie by Samuel Adamson   (0571 20442 2)
The Map Maker's Sorrow by Chris Lee   (0571 20365 5)
Silence by Moira Buffini   (0571 20445 7)
Bitter with a Twist by Simon Treves   (0571 20479 1)
My Dad's Corner Shop by Ray Grewal   (0571 20534 8)
Jump Mr Malinoff, Jump by Toby Whithouse   (0571 20584 4)
The Waiting Room by Tanika Gupta   (0571 20514 3)
Still Time by Stephanie McKnight   (0571 20782 0)
The Slight Witch by Paul Lucas   (0571 20935 1)
Behind the Scenes at the Museum by Bryony Lavery   (0571 20911 4)
A Wedding Story by Bryony Lavery   (0571 20906 8)
Belonging by Kaite O'Reilly   (0571 20902 5)